MENTALLY INCONTINENT

MENTALLY INCONTINENT

That Time I Burned Down a Hooters
That Time My Stalker Crashed on My Couch
and Nine Other Stories from My Weird Life

Joe Peacock

Gotham Books

GOTHAM BOOKS
Published by Penguin Group (USA) Inc.
375 Hudson Street, New York, New York 10014, U.S.A.
Penguin Group (Canada), 90 Eglinton Avenue East, Suite 700, Toronto, Ontario M4P 2Y3, Canada (a division of Pearson Penguin Canada Inc.); Penguin Books Ltd, 80 Strand, London WC2R 0RL, England; Penguin Ireland, 25 St Stephen's Green, Dublin 2, Ireland (a division of Penguin Books Ltd); Penguin Group (Australia), 250 Camberwell Road, Camberwell, Victoria 3124, Australia (a division of Pearson Australia Group Pty Ltd); Penguin Books India Pvt Ltd, 11 Community Centre, Panchsheel Park, New Delhi—110 017, India; Penguin Group (NZ), 67 Apollo Drive, Rosedale, North Shore 0632, New Zealand (a division of Pearson New Zealand Ltd); Penguin Books (South Africa) (Pty) Ltd, 24 Sturdee Avenue, Rosebank, Johannesburg 2196, South Africa

Penguin Books Ltd, Registered Offices: 80 Strand, London WC2R 0RL, England

Published by Gotham Books, a member of Penguin Group (USA) Inc.

First printing, November 2009
10 9 8 7 6 5 4 3 2 1

Gotham Books and the skyscraper logo are trademarks of Penguin Group (USA) Inc.

LIBRARY OF CONGRESS CATALOGING-IN-PUBLICATION DATA
Peacock, Joe.
    Mentally incontinent : that time I burned down a Hooters, that time my stalker crashed on my couch, and nine other stories from my weird life / Joe Peacock.
        p.   cm.
    ISBN 978-1-592-40482-7 (hardcover)
    1. Peacock, Joe—Anecdotes.   2. Peacock, Joe—Childhood and youth—Anecdotes.
3. Peacock, Joe—Humor.   4. American wit and humor.   5. Atlanta (Ga.)—Biography.
6. Young men—United States—Biography.   7. United States—Biography.   I. Title.
    CT275.P489A3   2009
    814'.54—dc22   2009027109

Printed in the United States of America
Set in Bembo
Designed by Elke Sigal

While the author has made every effort to provide accurate telephone numbers and Internet addresses at the time of publication, neither the publisher nor the author assumes any responsibility for errors, or for changes that occur after publication. Further, the publisher does not have any control over and does not assume any responsibility for author or third-party Web sites or their content.

Penguin is committed to publishing works of quality and integrity.
In that spirit, we are proud to offer this book to our readers;
however, the story, the experiences, and the words
are the author's alone.

DISCLAIMER

~~Everything I write is based on stuff from my life. I've lived through some pretty insane things, and this book is my attempt to either reconcile the tough memories or make people laugh with the silly ones. That said, the book is not a journalistic account of the events that have spanned the day I was born until now. I change names, I change descriptions, I embellish, and I spice up dialogue. This is a book, and it needs to be entertaining. So, with all of that said, if you get what I'm doing here—great. If you don't, and it makes you feel more comfortable, treat it like a work of fiction. Either way, as long as you laugh, my goals are satisfied.~~

I make everything up. It's all bullshit.

To Andrea:
my wife, best friend, and uncredited coauthor.
Without you, there's no book because there are no stories
worth telling. Thank you for being perfect.

FOREWORD

by

Drew Curtis,

founder and owner, Fark.com

I have lots of different kinds of bourbon at my house because people who come to Kentucky to visit me want to drink them.

My all-time favorite is Woodford Reserve Four-Grain. Only twelve thousand bottles of it were ever made. I have personally drunk over a dozen of them. If you want to know what it tastes like, think about all the pleasant flavors that might appear in bourbon (caramel, vanilla, etc.) combined with a finish that seems like it's going to kick you upside the head but never quite gets there. Even people who don't like bourbon like Four-Grain.

I introduced Joe to Four-Grain on one of his visits to Kentucky. He liked it so much he bought some to take back to Atlanta. One night he hit me on IM to tell me that he was drinking it and he thought he might be drunk, but he wasn't sure. I asked him how much of the bottle he'd had. His response: "Over half."

I assured him he was drunk. He was still uncertain until he tried to stand up, then he agreed with me.

I mention this because Joe's not a drinker. Otherwise he would have known to stop well before drinking most of an entire bottle of bourbon in one sitting. This is noteworthy because I often tell people that all good stories start with the immortal words "This one time I was really drunk." Very few if any of Joe's stories start with "This one time I was really drunk."

Some people are weirdness magnets. Joe Peacock is one of them.

It has been said that people who are lucky create their own luck. This implies that you can create your own luck. Joe Peacock creates his own weirdness. It's no mystery as to why these things happen to Joe. Joe can't let stuff go. By that I don't mean grudges or insults or the like; I mean that he can't leave alone ordinary stuff happening around him. He has to go poke it with a stick to see what happens. The results are often hilarious, although not necessarily at the time. Getting two nipple piercings ripped out, for example, was probably not hilarious at the time. I suspect the resulting nipple reconstruction surgery wasn't laugh-out-loud, either. Nor was seeing Joe in nipple casts for six weeks. (Actually, that was kinda funny.)

If Joe left stuff well enough alone, there wouldn't be any stories in this book. So thank God for Joe, who just has to go poke badgers with sticks, smack the shit out of beehives, and mess with people who generally deserve messing with. Without him, there would be far fewer funny stories.

INTRODUCTION

I can't say (with any honesty, anyway) that I ever thought
the day would come when a book by me would be published by a major publisher, stocked in bookstores, and purchased by people who could make other choices for reading
material.

I say this not because of a fundamental lack of confidence on my part but because I honestly thought that after
months of hearing me say, "Yes, the book is almost done,
just give me a little more time," my editor would come to
his senses and kick me to the curb.

Alas, he's too good a chap to do that. Thanks to him,
you have my book in your hands right now. So if you don't
like it, he's to blame. Well, he and about five thousand other
people, all of whom read, edited, and voted on the stories
that ended up in this thing. So if you have any complaints,
e-mail me and I'll pass them along to those responsible.

That's the one aspect that sets this book apart from many
others (besides the bitchin' cover). All of the material you're

reading was voted on by the readers of my Web site, www .mentallyincontinent.com. They edited them, offered suggestions on better wording, and otherwise kept me from sucking big-time. If this book entertains you in the slightest, it's because they made it work.

The truth is, I was (and am) very lucky to be doing the right thing at the right time. When I first started this whole book-on-the-Web nonsense in 2002, the Internet had already seen its first upheaval from the dot-com crash. Fresh ideas were rare, interest was low, and the world hadn't even heard the terms "social networking," "crowd sourcing," "Facebook," or "Paris Hilton video." That would all soon change.

A little program called Napster brought college students to the Web en masse in 2000. Shortly thereafter, when a whole lot of people got a whole lot of courage and began releasing a whole lot of stuff, for free, to the Net, they had an audience who was ready for it. It was very empowering to know that there was a way to "get out there" that no longer involved begging those with printing presses to put you in front of people. Even though the World Wide Web had been around since 1991, this delivery medium had become viable all of a sudden. And people began devouring everything they could find that was even slightly amusing.

That's where I come in. Which is to say, I was slightly amusing. And people, being the kind and sweet souls that they are, began reading my stories and supporting my efforts to build a book out of them and self-publish it. They voted on the ones they liked, and those stories became chapters in my first book. They then bought that book and had me draw stick figures on the front cover for an extra dollar added to the purchase price, and my hand went numb from drawing thousands of the little bastards.

Starting in 2006, I began writing the stories that would eventually be considered for the book you're holding now. Thanks to a fantastic community supporting my writing, the fifty or so stories I wrote and put on my site were whittled down to the best of the best. Good thing, too, because this is the big league. I'm *published*.

To try to start things off right, I thought I might continue a tradition started in the first book. I stole this idea from Neil Gaiman, who included an extra little story in the introduction to *Smoke and Mirrors*. It's a nice little reward for those of you who read the introductions to books. This is a story I liked that didn't get voted in.

A Leisurely Day Along the Mighty Merced

I've never been much of a beach guy, but I had to admit: This was nice.

It was just a sandy shoal along the banks of the Merced River in California, and that's probably why I was enjoying it so much.

On that small stretch of sand in the middle of Yosemite, I was lounging in a beached raft without a care in the world, with my wife of seven days, a sack lunch, and a bottle of local-grown orange juice purchased from a street vendor. It was probably eighty-nine degrees, and there was a gentle breeze blowing in from across the river. Birds chirped from the trees above us, and occasionally, a lizard scuttled across a rock in the distance and caught my eye.

There was a light yet constant note of laughter in the air from the families inhabiting the cabins that lined the bank of the river behind us. Fathers and daughters threw Frisbees while sons and mothers prepared lunches. Several happy couples had taken up picnicking spots not too close (yet not too far) from ours. The sun danced across the broken waters of the river.

I'd even forgotten about the blisters on my feet and the slight pull in my left hamstring from the sixteen-mile hike around the peaks of Yosemite a few days before. The lingering soreness was the reason we'd opted for a gentle Class 3 rafting excursion for our activity of the day. All it really called for was sitting in the raft, with an occasional need to put our oars in the water to keep us from bumping a rock now and again. And, of course, the two-hour lounge-across-your-raft-without-a-care-in-the-world lunch with my new bride.

Still sitting on the beach, I gently rolled my head to the left to find her sitting exactly as I was—legs hanging over the side of the raft, butt tucked inside, shoulders leaning across the stern, and arms lazily draped on the bow. As I looked at her admiringly, she turned her head to give me her own set of doting glances and smiles. She lightly reached up with her right hand and patted my left elbow as if to say,

"I am so glad we're here." I returned that sentiment with a big smile that said, "So am I."

Then came a rustle and a shout behind us. Andrea craned her neck up and backward to check it out. I rolled my hips toward her and twisted my head so I could get a glimpse myself. We saw two brown-skinned men running playfully toward the banks of the river, slapping and pushing each other all the while.

One was a younger, fit man with dark black hair and a bright white smile that could be seen from a hundred yards out. The other was an older man with a hairy belly and full beard, both sprinkled heavily with gray. It was immediately apparent that the two had entered into some informal, testosterone-laced wager to see who could beat the other in a race to the river and across it.

Andrea and I both whipped our heads around to follow them as they passed, sharing a chuckle at such a silly yet lighthearted moment between a family's two generations. Lord knows my father and I shared a number of these sorts of contests. Racing, arm wrestling, chess—there was hardly anything that we wouldn't turn into some form of competition. I reckon it's that way with all families, and usually, there comes a point when the younger student begins to outperform the older teacher, which was clearly the case here.

The younger man entered the river a full ten

paces ahead of his older relative. He looked sturdy and strong as he waded forward across the Merced and began swimming what was easily fifty yards to the other side. His pace was commanding and mighty; he pushed across the current of the rushing water with seeming ease.

His older relative was not quite so Grecian in his endeavors. He waded in with high knees, fighting the water as best he could. He practically belly-flopped into the shallows, and all of us watching muttered a sympathetic "Oooof!" He scraped into the heart of the river with all his might. To his credit, he put up a pretty good fight against this younger relative . . . until he ran out of gas.

He was about a third of the way across when he realized he wouldn't have enough steam to make it to the other side. He quickly stopped swimming and treaded water for a moment, turning to face our side of the shore, drifting downriver all the while. He began swimming as hard as he could toward us, apparently thinking it would be best if he could angle his return to the spot where he'd entered. Of course, he began floating downstream and ended up swimming as hard as he could to stay exactly where he was. When you're already out of gas, this is not exactly the best idea.

About five strokes into his return trip, swimming almost directly against the current, he went under. We all began to realize that this man was drowning right before our eyes.

I gasped. I shot up from inside the raft to get a better look. In the time it took me to get to my feet, my wife—a former swimming champion and lifeguard—was already diving headfirst into the river and kicking downstream to meet the man.

I was stunned. My first impulse was that Andrea was putting herself at risk, and I wanted to run to her and save her from this seductive river, which had already tricked one person into a false sense of serenity and was now attempting to kill him. But then I realized that was the issue: The river was trying to kill him, and he needed someone to save his life. My wife was not only strong and fit but qualified to do exactly that.

I'd seen her swim in competitions, so I knew just how fast she was. But somehow—either because of the river's current or because of the adrenaline spike (or both)—she seemed inhumanly fast as she stroked her way toward the drowning man. She arrived just as the man had taken what I counted to be his third gulp of air before he disappeared again (and possibly forever) under the frothy waters. Just as his head vanished, my wife's feet rose from the surface when she dove. They kicked once and then sank below for a moment.

As longtime readers know, I've had some pretty awful moments in my life. That was by far one of the worst—I thought she had been dragged below by the wailing and thrashing of this poor old man who had simply fallen victim to his own male pride.

My guts churned and I began to sweat. I couldn't feel the blisters on my feet or the strain in my pulled hamstring as I took a step toward the river. I had no idea what good it would do, but I was prepared to leap in after the pair of them. As I reached the edge of the water, Andrea reappeared with her arms wrapped around the portly gentleman.

Everyone on the banks of the river cheered.

She began sidestroking toward the beach with the man cradled in her right arm. I could see on her face that she was struggling. I ran back to the raft, grabbed my pocketknife, and cut the towrope tied to the bow of the craft. It was probably about twelve feet at most, but I thought maybe it could help.

I ran to the edge of the river and waded in as far as I could, slipping a bit here and there as my sandals made contact with the smooth rocks. I tossed the rope to my wife, who swam as hard as she could toward it. She made contact and grabbed on, and I pulled as hard as I could to drag her toward solid ground.

When their feet hit something solid, the man fell over, completely exhausted. He was coughing and gagging, physically begging for air. Andrea and I carried him over to the bank of the river and sat him upright, placing his arms over his head so he could get as much air as possible. She began softly coaching him to breathe slower, which helped him regain his breath.

Meanwhile, the younger man had arrived on the opposite side of the river and began checking to see by what margin he had beaten his older relative. He saw us standing around his competitor as the older man gasped and huffed. A look of panic overtook his face. He immediately dove back into the river and swam as hard as he could toward us.

Around the same time, the rest of their family rushed toward us. A middle-aged woman knelt down beside what I presumed was her husband and began hugging him and sobbing, reminding him all the while that he was "too *old* for this mess!" Several of the younger members of the family were thanking my wife for saving their relative's life. Other people on the banks were clapping and cheering.

When the younger man arrived back on our side of the river, the older woman left her almost-drowned husband and rushed to him. She began backhanding his chest and arms, yelling about how this was all his fault and how he knew better. The rest of the family helped the older man to his feet and guided him back to their cabin.

I gave my wife a huge hug and kiss. "That was an incredibly brave thing you just did," I said, impressed and dismayed simultaneously.

"Was it?" she asked. "I thought it was pretty stupid of me to do, myself. But hey, who else was going to do it?"

I knew, in that moment nearly six years ago, that

I had married the perfect woman—the only woman on the beach who could show up every guy there in terms of pure machismo.

So there you go, my first story in the big league. Here's hoping it (and the rest of the book) was worth your picking it up and reading it. Whether or not it was, I very much encourage you to let me know what you think of the book. Feel free to e-mail me anytime at joe@mentallyincontinent .com and share your thoughts, feelings, or recipes for curry— because I like hearing feedback on my work. It's the core of everything I do as a writer. You can also find my other Internet contact crap at the very back of the book. I hope you'll use it, because I'd like very much to be your BFF on Facebook and share Tweets on Twitter with you.

MENTALLY INCONTINENT

*If all else fails, immortality can always
be assured by spectacular error.*

—JOHN KENNETH GALBRAITH

CHAPTER 1

•

DOING THE GAY

I've always thought that, deep down inside, my mother harbors the thought that I might be, like . . . you know, *gay*.

A fairy. A poof. An other-side-of-the-fence dweller. I think she believes my relationship with my wife is simply a mask I use to cover up my deeply hidden desires to smoke poles. And what might give me the idea that my mother secretly thinks I prefer the company of men in matters romantic? Because at one point she not so secretly thought that I did. She even suggested to me that I was gay, openly and publicly.

Twice.

And I say "suggested" because, for my mother, being gay wasn't so much something she would "accuse" me of as something she felt the need to be encouraging and loving and supportive of; something she felt that—if I'd just relax and come clean and admit it—I might slip into and wear proudly and be all that much happier for it, like a silk bathrobe.

This all started with a vengeful and angry ex-girlfriend of mine named Mandy.

Now, the Mandy Situation was quite an interesting one. Mandy was a sweet girl. I need to make sure that's clear before I get into the story, because she really was sweet, and she probably deserved better than what she got.

I met Mandy through a mutual friend—the same friend I met my wife through, oddly enough—and just as quickly as I'm explaining it to you right now, I somehow ended up agreeing to take her to her senior prom.

"Hi."

"Hello."

"Prom?"

"Sure."

Just like that.

I didn't even go to my own senior prom, and somehow, two years after I graduated, I was rooked into going to Mandy's. Honestly, I don't remember who spoke which lines, except that I'm fairly certain she's the one who said "prom." I'm also fairly certain she's the one who said "sure." She may have said both the "hi" and the "hello." Such was the nature of Mandy: a sweet girl, to be sure.

Shortly after her prom (which was shortly after we met—so shortly, in fact, that my tuxedo ended up being cheaper to buy than to rent), we began "dating." She interpreted the term to mean "We will soon be getting engaged and then married and then I'll start spitting out babies in between my career as either a successful hotel chain owner/operator or a botanist—not sure which." I, however, took "dating" to mean "You're leaving for college at the end of the summer, and once you're gone, I'll be able to call you twice a month and send you some jewelry through the mail to fulfill my boyfriendly obligations." And that's precisely how it went, which was perfect for both of us. She got to feel like she had a man back home, and I got out of dating the weirdos I had been dating because I now had a girlfriend.

This went on for a little over a year. She'd come home twice a month and demand that I go shoe shopping with her or buy her some new clothes or scale a barbed-wire fence so we could go see the movie *Titanic*. The standard stuff a boyfriend is expected to do. Once those little manic forty-eight-hour periods were over, she'd drive back to college and I'd go back to playing the hot new game for the Sony PlayStation and building Web sites and generally trying to be by myself as much as possible.

Until one day, when a phone call came at nearly five in the morning.

"Guess what!" Mandy said excitedly.

"Uh . . . what?" I asked through a haze.

"Guess where I am!" she said in answer.

"Uh . . . where?" I said, unable to care.

"Look out your window."

Oh, no.

I did. Believe it or don't, she was there in her car, calling from her cell phone.

"Uh . . . hi?" I said. "Like . . . what are you doing here? It's Thursday."

"I just quit college!"

"You what?"

"Yeah, isn't that great!" she half asked, half didn't ask. "We can be together all the time now!"

Like I said, sweet girl. Clueless, demanding, smothering, clingy, a poor judge of other people's feelings toward her, and really bad at choosing her priorities. But very, very sweet.

"Yeah, uh . . . that's . . . mm . . . Hey, you want to hear what it sounds like when a relationship ends? It sounds like this—"

CLICK.

That was when the doorbell rang.

The worst part of what followed was that I didn't even get to break up with her in my own house. No. In an effort to be courteous to my housemates, I rode with her to a Waffle House to break up with her. When that didn't work, I rode with her to the park where we once spent a few hours, which held some sort of meaning to her, to break up with her. When that didn't work, I rode with her to her house to break up with her. Which was really smart, since she lived nearly an hour's drive away from my house.

Anyone who's had to walk the distance covered by an hour's drive can tell you that it sucks to walk it. But that night it was fine, because it gave me time to think about how awful the past day had been. It was a treat thinking about how she was nearly clawing my eyes out and calling me a name that, to her, probably made a whole lot of sense but really just sounded like every conjugation of the verb "fuck" and the noun "fuck" that could possibly be strung together at once, before she switched to literally clinging to my pants leg, begging me not to walk out the door. Again.

When I finally got home, I crawled back into bed. And I attempted to go back to sleep. And I succeeded for all of about twenty minutes. Until another phone call came.

"Hello?"

"Guess where I am."

Oh, no.

I walked out the door, right past her car, where she sat still clutching her cell phone, and got into my car and drove to the one place I knew she wouldn't dare to follow me: Mike's house.

My best friend, Mike, hated Mandy. Mandy hated Mike. It was a difficult situation until it became an ideal one. I knew I could sack out on his couch and not have to fear her sudden appearance, as Mike's mere presence struck a fearful chord within her and made her turn a ghostly shade of white.

In retaliation, she went to the one place she felt she could try to get me back. She went to my mom's house. And she stayed for nearly twelve hours a day, every day, for a solid week. At first it was simple demands.

"Mrs. Peacock, you've got to help me get Joe back!"

Then it turned into very long and drawn-out laments.

"Mrs. Peacock, why won't Joe come back?"

From there, she began spiraling down, beginning with examinations of her character and what possibly could have driven me away, and turning to examinations of my character and what possibly could have made me want to leave. And that was where the correlations were drawn.

At the end of the week, I called my mother to find out if the coast was clear—which it was—and I went over to mow the grass. There I was confronted by one of the most surreal conversations I've ever had with anyone at any time whatsoever.

"What's this about?" I asked in response to my mother's request that I take a seat at the dining room table.

"Joe, honey," she said, taking a seat across from me, "I want to go ahead and say right up front that I love you."

"I love you, too, Mom," I replied with a queer look in her direction.

"I mean it," she reaffirmed. "No matter what you ever do or say, I will always love and support you."

"That's . . . That's really great, Mom . . ."

"And if you want to have a relationship with Mikey—"

"What?" I said, taken aback. I narrowed my eyes and spoke very slowly. "In what context, exactly, do you mean the word 'relationship' to be taken in this instance, Mother?"

"Well . . . you know . . . like . . . if you and Mikey are . . . gay. Together."

"Gay together!" I shouted, nearly as perplexed that she would think her girl-chasing son of twenty years would be homosexual despite overwhelming evidence to the contrary as I was at the fact that she actually said "gay *together*."

"Son," she said, "I know all about it, and it's okay. Your father and I accept the fact that—"

"What!" I couldn't believe this. "You told Dad that I was gay?"

"Well, I didn't," she replied. "Mandy did."

Sweet girl, that Mandy. Misguided, in denial, absolutely psycho, and completely off the reservation. But sweet. Very, very sweet.

"Mom," I said, clearly and distinctly. "I want you to tell me exactly what she said."

"Basically, she said—"

"No, Mom. Not basically. I want to know *exactly* what she said."

"Here, you can read it for yourself," she replied, and stood up to go and fetch a letter. A letter from Mandy.

A twenty-two-page letter from Mandy, which conveyed in rather excruciating detail first how much she loved me, second how much I'd broken her heart, third how gay I was with Mike, and fourth how that was the only explanation behind the dissolution of our relationship because what we had was REAL and PURE and only something like DEVIANT SEXUAL BEHAVIOR could possibly pull the two of us apart.

And what was the evidence she had to substantiate my desire to place my penis in the anal crevasse of my good friend?

1. At one point she asked me, if Mike moved somewhere like Seattle, would I go with him. To which I answered yes.

2. She thought my need to constantly punch him in the shoulder was born of an innate desire to place my hands on his penis. This was supported by a passage she read in *Details* magazine, photocopied and given to the students of a Psych 101 class she'd taken the year before.

3. I went to his house after we broke up. She knew this because she followed me over there.

4. I hugged him upon his return from a three-week trip to his home city of Detroit.

5. We were always calling each other "dick" and "penis."

"Mom . . ." I said, tossing the letter aside and propping my right cheek on my right palm.

"Now you see?" she asked. "I know all about it. And it's okay—we support you." Then she hugged me.

It could have been worse. She could have hated me based on these incredibly ludicrous and absolutely disjointed pieces of evidence that I wanted to make beastly, sweaty love to my hairy and rather stinky best friend.

The other long, drawn-out talk about my sexual orientation came shortly after I had my nipples pierced on a bet.

I went over to my parents' place to help pack away the January snowman decorations and pull down the February Valentine's decorations and, in the midst of everything, got rather sweaty and needed to shower before I went out on a date (with a girl). Since I had been living on my own for a while, I'd forgotten about closing the bathroom door to hide things from my parents. So after the shower, I was shaving my face with the door open and a towel around my waist when my mother walked by and saw the little silver hoops hanging from my teats.

"OH MY GOD!"

"What?" I said, wincing from having cut myself due to her outburst.

"You really are gay!" she cried.

"Wait, what?"

"You have nipple piercings!" she announced. "Only the gays have nipple piercings!"

"Well, no, Mom, that's not necessarily true," I responded. "Guys who take stupid bets have them, too."

Because I really had to get ready quickly and meet my date, I didn't get to battle with her about my non-homosexuality. Which left her with the indelible impression that I was, very clearly, doing the gay. With men. And not women, like the one I was going to meet.

It took a long-term relationship that subsequently resulted in marriage to convince my dear sweet mother that I was (and am), in fact, not gay. When I think back on it, I want to think that she was eager for me to admit to her that I was gay so she could prove to me how supportive and loving she really is. Knowing I could count on my mommy to be there to support and love me makes me love her dearly.

I'm just glad I didn't have to plow man-butt to find that out.

CHAPTER 2

NEVER SAW
THAT ONE COMING . . .

"**D**ude. Come on," he pleaded, sighing and shaking his head.

I refused to look up at him. "I said no, Mike."

"Look, all I'm saying . . ." He sighed again. "Hey—could you hit pause or something?"

"Don't want to."

"I don't care if you want to," he answered. "Just do it, okay?"

I stared at the screen. Thinking about the situation now, I realize I shouldn't have bothered. I should have ignored his request and gone right on playing *Mario64*. But at the time, the fact that my best friend in the world was standing in the doorway to my room, practically begging me to listen to him, won me over and made me do the courteous thing.

"There," I said as I pushed the start button, "it's paused. I have paused my game because you asked me to."

"Good," he said.

"Yes, good," I echoed. "Now I can devote my complete and undivided attention to ignoring you."

We stared at each other for about fifteen seconds—which doesn't sound like much when you're reading about it, but if you ever try it, you'll find that fifteen seconds is quite a long time to stare at somebody. After that time had passed, he sighed once more, turned on his left foot, and groaned as he pretended to leave my doorway in frustration.

"Yes, fine," I said, unpausing my game. "Leave. Mario and I are having fun without you."

"No no no no," said Mike as he grudgingly returned to my doorway. "It's not fine. You need to get back out there."

I simply continued playing the game.

"Look," he said, "it's been three weeks since she left."

I stopped moving the joystick, and I stopped mashing buttons. I turned to him and sternly asked, "So?"

"So she hasn't even called you, Joe." He came into the room and stood in front of the television.

The whole Katherine Thing had become a massive point of contention between me and my little circle of friends (which included my future wife). I wanted nothing more than to forget it ever happened. And they wanted nothing more than to remind me how big a mistake I'd made.

"I know, Mike. You don't have to remind me. And you certainly don't have to stand in front of my game while doing so."

"Come on, this will be good for you," he replied. "You need to get out there and get back in the saddle."

"She's going to wear a saddle?" I asked. "Kinky."

He stared at me. "You're an ass." He made his way over the cord of the controller and plopped onto my couch.

"Yup," I answered, scooting over slightly to make room.

"Katherine doesn't love you, Joe," he said.

I looked at him.

"She never did," he reiterated.

I looked back at the screen. Mario had lain down on the ground and begun taking a nap due to the lack of attention I was paying him. "Yeah, I know."

"So."

"So?"

"So why don't you just get past it?" he asked.

"It's not that easy," I answered.

"Sure it is," he said. "You just take every letter and e-mail and whatever that she wrote, dump them, and move on with your life."

"Oh." I glanced his way. "That's all, huh? Shit, where have you been all this time? Damn it all to hell!" I yelled. "Here I've been, like an idiot, suffering through this shit. And all I had to do was throw away some paper and delete a few e-mails!" I turned my attention back to the game, jiggling the stick and waking my plumber from his slumber.

He stood up. "Fine. Stay here and sulk, you dick. Skip out on an opportunity to meet someone new and maybe have a good time."

"Okay," I replied unemotionally. "I sure will."

He navigated himself over the cord of the controller again and headed toward the door. "I don't know why you have to be such a baby about it."

"Who's being a baby?" I asked rhetorically. "I don't go on blind dates. You know that."

"What?" he said with a sarcastic chuckle. "You don't call taking a trip to Savannah with a girl you met on the Internet a blind date?"

"No," I answered, "I've known her for—"

"For a week," he interrupted. "I don't care how long you chatted with her on your little chat program thing, you actually *knew* her for a week."

"Get out," I demanded. "Go meet your girlfriend and my blind date and get the fuck out of here."

"Fine," he answered as he marched out of the room. "You should know, however, that Rachel says she's totally hot."

"Don't care," I replied as I maneuvered Mario around the stage, then suddenly brought him to a standstill. "Wait— how hot?"

"I dunno," he said, pausing in the middle of the room. "Hot."

"Like Rachel hot? Because if she's Rachel hot, I'm not interested."

"Dude," he said, "that's my girlfriend you're talking about."

"Yeah," I said, "and I hate her."

"Yeah," he answered, knowing this to be true. "Still, show some courtesy, huh?"

"Sure, okay." I paused the game once again so I might pay total attention to Mike the Matchmaker. "The question remains—how hot?"

"I dunno. Rachel said she's really pretty."

"Pretty?" I sneered. "Pretty isn't hot, dude."

"Hot, okay? She said hot."

"How hot?"

He shrugged. "She didn't say."

"Have you seen her?" I asked.

"No."

"Bah," I answered, turning back to the game.

Mike left the room only to return under a minute later with his cordless phone in hand. "Hey," he said into the receiver as he sat next to me once again. "He wants to know how hot."

I heard some buzzing over the earpiece.

"Here," he said, thrusting the phone in my face. "She wants to talk to you."

"Who?" I said, placing the phone between my ear and shoulder.

"She's really hot," Rachel said from the other end of the phone.

"Like Cindy Crawford hot?" I said, realizing immediately who it was.

"Hotter," she replied.

I chuckled a little. "Right. Just like *Scream* was a great movie," I said, throwing her opinions back at her.

"It was!" she yelled. "You have no taste in movies!"

"I have impeccable taste in movies," I replied, "and you liked *Scream*—AND you're dating Mike. The combination of those two things calls into question your judgment concerning any and all matters of taste."

"Hey!" Mike said, elbowing me and causing me to jostle

the controller and send Mario over the side of a cliff and into an eternal abyss.

"Great job, fuckhead," I said. "That was my last guy!"

"You deserve it," Rachel said. "Besides, you shouldn't be playing video games while talking to me on the phone. It's rude."

"Well, I don't like you," I said in reply. "So, you know, fuck that."

"Fuck you, too," she said. "Look—go out with my cousin tonight."

"No," I said, tossing the controller toward the Nintendo 64 and lifting myself off the couch. "I'm not interested, okay? I don't want to, you know, get back on the bike or whatever it is Mike thinks I should do."

"Saddle," Mike corrected. "Get back in the saddle."

"You know, that metaphor doesn't make sense. It doesn't even apply to me. I don't even know how to ride a horse," I said.

"You would if you got back in the saddle," he said.

I stared blankly at him.

"Are you going to go out with her tonight?" Rachel asked from her end of the phone.

"No," I replied. Then something sparked in my mind. "Wait—why the hell do you guys want me to go out with her so bad? What, does she just need a man in her life or something?"

"Tonight she does," Mike said under his breath as Rachel began to answer my question.

I covered the receiver of the phone with my hand. "What does that mean?" I whispered to Mike.

"You want the truth?" he asked.

"Yeah, of course," I said, with Rachel's voice still buzzing in the earpiece.

"Her cousin's in town because her parents and Rachel's parents are in Florida for the weekend," he said. "Some sort of adult-getaway weekend thing."

"So?" I said, ignoring the phone.

"So, with Rachel's parents out of town, that gives us the house for the evening . . ."

"Oh," I said, with a tiny little bell going off in my head. "This is about you getting laid."

"Well, no. Wait. Yes but no. You need to get back out there and start seeing people, man."

"Hey, don't turn this into a 'me' thing, you asshole!" I barked. "You wanna get laid? Just say so."

"B-but—" he stammered.

"No buts—you need a wingman, so be honest. Just say 'I need you to babysit the cousin while I try to get into my prude girlfriend's pants.'"

"Oh my God, what did you say?" I heard Rachel say from the earpiece.

I realized I'd taken my hand off the receiver to point at Mike for emphasis, leaving it open for Rachel to hear our conversation. "Uhh . . ." I said, "I said . . . uh . . ."

"I heard what you said," she replied. "Why do you have to be so crass?"

"Why do you have to be such a damn prude?" I said, turning it back on her.

"I'm not a prude!" she yelled.

"You're not?" I asked as Mike buried his face in his

hands. "Then how come you won't just come over here, where you are one hundred percent free of parental supervision, and get it on?"

"God," she said, sounding embarrassed. "See what I mean? Crass! I can't deal with you guys hearing us!"

"So you'd rather do it in the backseat of a Jeep?"

"Oh my God, he told you about that?" she screamed.

"Of course," I answered, watching Mike's entire body turn red. "He tells me everything."

A muffled noise echoed through the phone, sounding almost like a balloon releasing air through its tightly pulled neck. "I cannot *believe* you two!" Rachel said once she was done squealing.

"Yeah, whatever," I said with a sigh. "You know what? Fine. You guys want me to entertain your cousin, I'll entertain your cousin. Whatever. I don't care. She just better not be ugly."

"She's not," Rachel said. "I promise."

"Or stupid," I added.

"No, she's really smart," she countered.

"Okay," I said, and hung up the phone.

Mike looked at me. "You just hung up on her?"

"Yup," I answered, tossing his phone back to him.

"You'll be hearing about that one later," he said.

"Oh, I imagine," I said, moving past him. "What time are we meeting them, then?"

"Eight," he replied. "At Outback. Be ready in an hour."

"An hour?" I asked. "It's only five o'clock, dude. We only live, like, ten minutes from Outback."

"Gotta make a stop first," he replied.

I looked at him quizzically for a second. He pointed at his crotch. I immediately caught on and nodded.

For the normal human being, the acquisition of prophylactics should be a two-minute operation, if not quicker. You walk in, you grab a box, you pay, and you go. However, Mike being Mike, the extra hour and twenty minutes was necessary because he needed time to evaluate every product, analyzing both strengths and features of each individual cut of condom. Because of this, a gas station or convenience store was out of the question. We would most likely have to stop at Wal-Mart on the way.

That was fine by me; I figured on visiting the electronics section and fiddling with the televisions on display.

An hour later, he burst into my room and asked, "Are you ready to go?"

"Yeah," I replied while continuing to play *Mario64.* "Just gotta get my shoes on."

I felt him looking at me from across the room. I looked over at him—he was wearing slacks, a button-down oxford, and a curious look on his face. "Is that what you're wearing?" he asked, pointing at my New York Rangers jersey and accompanying Levi's.

"Uh, yeah," I answered. "Is that what you're wearing?"

"Yeah," he snapped. "It's a date!"

"Yeah? So?"

"So . . ." he answered, trying to tie his necktie. "Don't you, you know, want to make a good impression?"

"No, not really."

His face grew red. "Look, if you don't want to do this, I'd prefer you just say so and stay home."

"Really?" I asked with my eyes wide as platters. "What happened to the first two hundred times I said no? Or what about when I said 'hell no' and 'fuck that' and—"

"Just . . ." he started. "You know what . . . fine. Just . . . go put on a tie and let's go."

"I'm not wearing a tie," I said, finally guiding Mario to the level in the game I'd been trying to get to for the past hour.

"Yes, you are," he replied, switching off the console.

"Hey! I didn't even get to save, you asshole!"

"Get up!" he barked.

"Fine." I marched over to my closet. It took all of two minutes for me to throw on a pair of khakis and a button-down shirt that halfway matched. Then we ran out the door so he could pick just the right style of rubber for his clandestine coital rendezvous.

Because of my ability to bypass his insane shopping ritual and simply grab a pack off the shelf and buy it, we arrived at Outback nearly an hour earlier than necessary. When we were faced with the question of what we should do in the meantime, my vote of "go the fuck home" was discounted on the basis that I was not the one in control of the vehicle that evening. Instead, at my behest, we elected to go in and have a few drinks.

"But you don't drink," he said in reply to my alternate suggestion.

"I'm starting tonight."

Inside the restaurant, we gave the hostess our names and waited about two minutes for a seat, which ended up being in plain view of a television showing a New York Rangers game. We became absorbed in the game. Well, Mike did, anyway. I mostly watched the guys in the blue shirts chase the puck across the ice while thinking about Katherine and that great week we shared. And the nature of our relationship (if you could call it that). I thought a lot about the things Mike had said—that maybe I did deserve a chance at happiness, and that maybe what Katherine and I'd had was fleeting and temporary.

I thought about how this evening could be the start of something special for me. It could open the door to a brand-new outlook. I could be starting down a new path with a new person, you know? She might be just what I was looking for. Maybe Rachel wasn't lying when she said this girl was pretty and smart. Maybe this girl was a total 10 and I'd be lucky if she'd have me. Maybe khakis and a collared shirt were called for this evening.

"Hi, guys," I heard a familiar voice say from in front of me.

"Hey!" Mike said, shooting out of his chair to hug and kiss his girlfriend.

"Hey," I said, looking in the direction of Mike and Rachel. I could see someone standing behind them, but I couldn't make out who it was or what she looked like. "You're blocking the game," I said curtly.

Rachel turned her head away from Mike's cheek and looked at me. "Rude," she snapped.

"So is blocking my view of the game," I answered with a smirk. "Where's my date?"

Mike was also looking my way, his eyes the size of platters. I guessed he'd gotten a look at my date for the evening.

He was mouthing something to me, but I couldn't make out what it was.

Rachel smiled. "Nice to see you've warmed up to the idea of meeting her, Joe." She broke from Mike, who stepped to the side to let Rachel's cousin walk forward and meet me. "Joe, this is Jennifer," Rachel said cheerfully.

Just then I heard crowd noise from the television screen. Someone had scored a goal. I couldn't be bothered to check who it was. My eyes were fixed on my blind date. "Well, now, isn't *this* interesting," I said as she came into view.

Now, for all intents and purposes, Jennifer was great. Her sense of style was very fashionable and current—I recognized quite a few labels on her clothing as some of the premier fashion ambassadors of the day. She had beautiful, almost shining blond hair that reminded me of the windswept fields of golden wheat that adorn the middle section of this great and glorious nation. Her eyes were as serene and innocent a blue as I had seen up to that point in my life, and her smile, bright as a shore beacon, lit up the room. There was just one teeny, tiny little problem.

"How old are you?" I blurted out before we could even exchange pleasantries.

She withdrew her outstretched hand. "Uh . . . fifteen," she responded, slightly startled at my bluntness.

My head whipped sharply left to face Mike and Rachel, who wore shocked and unaffected expressions, respectively. "Are you fucking *kidding* me?" I whispered in their direction. Mike's mouth hung open.

"What's the problem?" Rachel asked.

"What can I get you to drink?" the server with the poor sense of timing said from behind me.

We all slowly sank into our unassigned seats and politely went through the paces of ordering our drinks. Without thinking of decorum or manners, I blurted out, "I'll have a sweet tea."

"Root beer," Mike requested.

The server wrote down what the unchivalrous men had ordered. "And for the ladies?"

"I'll have a Zima," Rachel said.

"That sounds good—I'll have one of those, too!" Jennifer said.

"Uh . . ." Mike said, looking at Rachel, who winked at him a few times.

"You can't order that," I said to Jennifer.

"*Yes I can,*" she said through clenched teeth, indicating that I was blowing her cover. "You didn't, like, order it *for* me, so I had to order it myself."

"She's, uh . . . not driving tonight," Rachel added, attempting to play things cool. "So yeah, go ahead and order it, Jen Jen. I'll buy." Rachel was giving me a look that said, "We're totally going to go through with this, and you're a total asshole if you rat her out."

I looked at Rachel in much the way my mother would look at my father when he allowed me to do things I shouldn't, like ride four-wheelers or look at *Playboy*. "She's not old enough to have a license, much less drink!" I snapped.

Rachel and I held each other's stare as the server read

off the list of beverages we'd ordered. "All right, I have a tea, a root beer, and a Zima," she said as she raised her head and looked at me. "And I'll just bring your . . . uh, date . . . a Coke," she said with a smile as she closed her little notepad and walked away.

"You ass!" Rachel said, scowling at me.

Jennifer punched me. I turned to face her. She was angry. And fifteen.

"You know what?" I said. "I really gotta, like, piss or something. Come on, Mike."

"You need him to piss?" Rachel asked. "What, you need him to hold it for you or something?"

"Yup," I replied, "it's that big. Mike, let's *go*."

Dutifully, Mike stood and followed me to the restroom.

"Dude, come on," Mike said for what must have been the hundredth time.

I stopped pacing the tile floor of Outback's luxurious men's restroom and stared hard at him. "Mike, I do *not*," I yelled, pausing for effect before "want to hear it."

"Hey, don't get pissy with me! It's not *my* fault!"

"No?" I asked. "Who was it who said 'Get back in the saddle, Joe!' and 'You can't hide in your room forever, Joe!' It certainly wasn't *me*!"

"Aw, come on! How was I supposed to know she was only fifteen? I'd never seen her before! How the hell can you blame *me*?"

I thought for a moment. "*Fuck!*" I yelled, slamming the backs of my shoulders against the wall and covering my face with my hands.

"Hey, maybe you could yell that a little louder!" Mike suggested. "I don't think everyone in the restaurant heard it."

"It doesn't matter now, does it? They all think I'm a pedophile anyway—they might as well think I'm a foul-mouthed pedophile."

"Oh, come on. You are totally overblowing this!"

"Am I? Dude, I'm twenty-one years old—and I look nearly thirty."

"Well, not really thirty," Mike interjected. "The beard does make you look older, but only, like, twenty-five."

"That doesn't help, Mike!" I yelled. "Did you not see the server's expression when she took our drink order?"

"What about it?"

"She looked at me like I was the dirtiest man alive!"

"Oh, she did not," he replied with a sigh. "You're just paranoid."

"Well, you're an asshole."

He looked at me, registering my statement. He knew I was right, and he knew that even though he really, really wanted me to let all of this stuff go and make it through the night so he could score with his girl, he was pushing it. If he tried to keep me involved in this evening's events, he would be going far beyond asking for a favor. He would be leaning on our friendship to get what he wanted.

Without a sigh, or a dampened tone of voice, or any other signals betraying his earnestness, he said very honestly, "Dude, we can go home right now if you want. We will walk out of this bathroom, hit the car, and I'll make up with Rachel later. Just say the word, and we're outta here."

I thought about it. I heard what he was saying—and

believe me, I wanted to take him up on that offer. I wanted nothing more than to bolt out of there and be clear of the possibility that people might see me and think of me as some sort of Camaro-driving predator who lusted after teenage girls. But there was something much larger at stake.

There was a favor owed.

Almost a year ago to the day, Mike had done one of the greatest things a friend could ever do for another friend. I'd been on a trip with Mandy, for whom I'd once ensnared myself in barbed wire. We were in Myrtle Beach during spring break, and Mandy got it in her head that she was going for a walk on the beach. She wanted me to come along. I agreed and took off my shirt. She got all embarrassed and refused to go out with me.

I asked her at least twenty times to explain before I got her to confess—I was too pale and had a bit of a tummy. Not too big of one . . . just too big to look good among the college spring breakers partying up and down the beach.

To be fair, she had a point—a materialistic, stuck-up bitch can't be seen with an average guy. But all the same, I called my good friend Mike to come pick me up. He drove all the way from Atlanta—a six-hour drive—without even questioning me.

Mike did it without complaining, not even once. He just said, "All right," hopped in the car, and came and picked me up. And he never once threw it in my face or even reminded me that he'd done it. He was way too good a friend to ever pull the old "You owe me one" out of the closet.

That made it doubly hard to avoid paying him back for favors. I knew that, with enough grit and determination, I could survive the evening and babysit the cousin while Mike and his girlfriend attempted to get it on.

I sighed. "I'm going to regret this . . . but no. I'll stay."

"Thankyouthankyouthankyou," he said, half hugging me.

"Dude, it's no big . . . Well, yeah, it is a big deal. Let's just get it over with."

"I owe you one," he said as we turned to walk out.

"Nope, we're even," I corrected. "So hey, how long has it been since—"

"Two weeks," he answered immediately as he pushed the door open.

"Really," I said. "Why?"

"Parents caught us," he said. "She won't even kiss me in the house now."

"Pathetic."

"Mmm-hmm," he muttered. "And when was your last time?"

"This isn't about me," I said nonchalantly as we reached our table.

"What isn't about you?" Rachel asked. "Manners?"

"Twat," I answered.

"Oh, it must be respect, then. Is respect not about you?" she asked. "You're damn rude, you know that?"

"I do," I answered, placing my napkin in my lap.

"Joe was just sharing with me how long it's been since he's had sex," Mike said to the table.

"Oh?" asked Rachel. "And how long has it been, Joe?"

"I did stumble across those risqué ads for escorts in the back of *Creative Loafing* a few days ago," I replied. "Does solo count?"

"Ew," Jennifer replied. "That's just nasty."

"Just wait until you hit puberty, you might change your mind," I said sharply.

"At least four months," Mike said abruptly.

We looked at him, all of us with the same expression, which read, "What?"

"It's been at least four months since you last had sex," Mike answered.

"Wow," I said. "It's amazing how well you keep a topic alive, no matter how much I wish it would die."

"I'm just saying."

"Just STOP saying," I replied, taking a sip from my—ugh!—unsweetened tea. "Nasty! She brought me unsweetened," I said with a grossed-out face.

"Matches your demeanor," Rachel quipped, rolling her eyes.

I tried to watch the Rangers game, but it was hard. Mostly because watching would mean staring right above Rachel's head, and each time I tried to get into the game, she would look at me and I'd look at her and she'd scowl and I'd scowl and my focus would be broken and I'd have no choice but to look off to my right (since Jennifer was to my left and I wasn't interested in looking in her direction at all). But I'd get bored with looking at the wall and the door to the kitchen and eventually look back up at the game, which would cause Rachel to look at me, and so on.

"So, everyone ready to order?" the server said when she finally returned to our table.

We were. In fact, I don't think any of us at that table had ever been more ready for anything in our lives. We all wanted to order our food, eat it, and get the hell out of there as quickly as possible. Mike and Rachel for obvious reasons; Jennifer because it was probably already past her bedtime; and me because I'd been set up on a blind date with a fifteen-year-old.

We ordered our respective meals and proceeded to eat them while Rachel and Jennifer chatted about purses and cute boys and really bad music, Mike and Rachel chatted about really bad music, and Mike and Jennifer chatted a little about what she liked to do (go to the mall), what her favorite band was (Backstreet Boys), and what her favorite book was ("I don't, like, read and stuff"). I just sat there and watched the New York Rangers lose.

I let my cold exterior melt a bit and even managed to engage both Jennifer and Rachel in conversation that didn't include some form of insult. It was hard, but I'm a soldier. I was built for this. Plus, my molars were beginning to throb from all the teeth-grinding I was doing.

So dinner was awkward. But it was nothing compared to the movie.

We went to see *Urban Legend*—Jennifer's choice, backed by Rachel (and apparently Mike, since he offered no argument against it). I was in hell, because I can't stand modern horror films. It wasn't three minutes into the "film" when I looked over at my best friend to share a knowing smile about how stupid the opening scene was, only to find him shoving his tongue into his girlfriend's mouth like a face-hugger trying to impregnate a colonial marine. With a sigh, I sank into my chair and started watching twenty-four frames per second of utter dreck.

And then a ridiculously corny yet super-scary scene happened. I felt a hand grab my forearm and a nose bury itself into the little joint between my bicep and my chest. I heard Jennifer yelp from deep in my armpit. She looked up at me with a face full of earnestness. "That was *so* scary!" she whispered.

"Mm-hmm," I replied, turning back to the movie.

I began counting the seconds after I turned away from her that she left her hand on my arm. I couldn't help it. It was because she was fifteen and I was creeped the hell out. I wanted to yank my arm away. I really, really wanted to. And I would have, but I didn't want to be flat-out mean. So, I figured, I'd count to about thirty or forty and then stretch a little, releasing her grip and making it look like I had a real reason to knock her off me. I'd gotten up to about thirty-two seconds when another super-scary scene appeared. I again felt her head bury itself in my armpit. I felt her hand squeeze, and I again looked down at her. Again she looked up at me. This time she did not yelp or whisper how scary the scene was. No. This time she reached up to kiss me.

"Gah!" I yelled. I immediately flinched back. She reached my face in time to plant her lips on the base of my jaw.

"Allrighty," I announced, pulling my arm away and standing up, "that's the evening for me."

Mike yanked his tongue out of his girlfriend's mouth long enough to mutter, "Dude."

"Nope," I said, sliding past him and Rachel and reaching the stairs, "I'm out. That's it."

"But—"

I didn't even hear what he said. Someone three rows behind us elevated the natural volume of his voice to remind us that there was a movie going on, he had paid for it, and if we'd be so kind as to shut up, he would much appreciate it.

I lifted my hand and waved at my friend, his girlfriend, and the little kid they'd stuck me with, all without turning to face them. I'd managed to exit the door when I heard Mike from behind me.

"Dude, seriously—how are you going to get home?"

"Walk," I said, not holding the door for Mike as I left the theater.

"I can't let you walk," he said from the open doorway. "It's freezing out there!"

"I'll be fine," I said, walking backward so I could see him. "Don't let that door close, you'll have to buy another ticket." I turned back around, almost performing a full walking 360.

"Dude," he mumbled again.

I heard the door close. "Enjoy the evening," I said to my friend who had left me to walk home alone.

"What do you mean?" he asked from behind me.

I turned in shock. "You idiot! You're going to have to buy another ticket to get in there, you know."

"Nah," he said, "I'm not going back in."

"But—"

"If you leave, I'm leaving," he said. "I'm not going to have this on my conscience all night."

"If I stay, I'm going to have to hang around a fifteen-year-old who's been trying to molest me all night!" I said. "You'll have that on your conscience instead."

"Nah," he said, "let's go."

I looked at him for a moment. "What about having the house to yourself tonight?"

"There'll be other opportunities," he said as he began walking to the car.

"But . . ." I said, beginning to feel like an incredible ass as I chased after him. "Shit. I'm totally screwing you over, aren't I?"

"No," he said, "we should have left the second she brought a kid as your date. You're not screwing me over." He stopped walking and turned to face me. "It took a real friend to even put up with that. Thanks."

He smiled a little and then turned to walk to the car. I smiled a little myself and followed him.

Two days later, Rachel forgave Mike and came over to the house we shared. She'd apparently gotten over her phobia of "doing it" with the housemates present because Mike's stereo boomed far louder than it needed to all night.

Not that THAT was what kept me up . . . I had old letters to throw away and some e-mails to delete.

CHAPTER 3

THE HOSPITAL IS NO PLACE
TO SPEND YOUR BIRTHDAY

I have the world's worst birthdays.

This is not hyperbole thrown out to gain sympathy or win some sad game in which one earns credit for being the most pathetic. It's merely a point of fact. It's not even a co-incidence at this point, or the by-product of self-fulfilling prophecy. It seriously does not matter what I do—I can leave town, I can wear lucky charms . . . hell, I can eat Lucky Charms, and it has no effect. One birthday I locked myself in a room with a stack of DVDs and enough food to last the day. When I finally turned the phones back on, I got a call saying that the appeal my wife and I had filed on a five-year lawsuit regarding the property line of our house had been lost, thus flushing away nearly forty-five thousand dollars we'd spent trying to get the original owners to admit they'd lied to us.

The birthday curse finds me no matter where I go or what I do. But it produces some pretty insane stories. Now, there hasn't been a birthday in my life that wasn't rife with some sort of insane something-or-other, but there are five that really jump out and beg to be talked about, mostly because all of them took place in the same location: the emergency room.

It was my twenty-fourth birthday. I looked up in time to see the clock tick through the three seconds it needed to officially be two o'clock in the morning. It was a chore to even breathe, and the antiseptic smell of the hospital burned my nostrils with each breath. I pondered the concept that after nearly four hours of exposure, one would expect the nostrils and lungs to be adjusted to the burn and odor of the iodine in the air. I concluded that if one assumed this, one was clearly very, very wrong. With that realization, I exhaled a deep sigh.

It wasn't a sigh of resignation, which I'd sighed around one o'clock that morning. And it wasn't a sigh of frustration, which I'd sighed at midnight. No, this was simply one of those meaningless sighs you exhale to pass the time: a mental marker that the moment has come and gone when what little hope that you might ever see a doctor has at last expired.

Mike looked over and half smirked, half frowned at me, indicating that he, too, had just experienced the mourning of an unanswered prayer. I shrugged in response and shifted my weight slightly, allowing the chair to numb a different buttock for a while. As I did, a pair of young, hyperenergetic children raced past where we sat, slightly jostling my left elbow.

I winced in response to the jolt that shot through my

left hand and tore through my body. I gritted my teeth to keep from yelping like a hobbled puppy. I gripped my left wrist tightly in an effort to keep the pounding in my veins from reaching the spot in the meaty part of my left hand where approximately two thirds of an X-Acto knife blade rested in its impromptu home. The white gauze pad lightly taped across the entry wound began to grow red as the over-worked platelets at the wound site said, fuck it, shrugged, and gave up working to keep the damn cut from bleeding all over the place.

Mike noticed my reaction and was about to offer both his concern for my well-being and any services he could perform to help me in the situation, but just as he opened his mouth, an ambulance's siren began blaring outside the window where we sat. Mike's orange-marker-covered face immediately squinted tight as he cupped his ears with his orange-marker-covered hands. Instinctively, I raised my black-marker-covered hands to do the same, but as soon as I lifted my black-marker-and-blood-covered hand, another jolt of pain shot through my arm.

I winced. Without even thinking about it, I re-placed the right hand that had gone to protect my right ear back on my left wrist, which clearly needed the aid more than my poor eardrums. The ambulance sped away, taking its blaring siren with it, which was good. As it got out of earshot, a small baby who had fallen asleep on his redneck mother's over-size breast awoke and decided to take up the ambulance's challenge on who could blow out the most eardrums. He let loose with both barrels.

I'd thought that my eyes were already shut as tightly as they could be, but somehow I was able to squeeze out a tiny bit more light. Another sigh escaped my lungs so quickly, I couldn't determine what kind of sigh it was. The throbbing in my hand made its way up my arm and into my brain as my head began pounding with the warning signs of an oncoming migraine.

I opened my eyes to find one of the small children who'd run past earlier standing beside my chair and looking over my outstretched left palm. "Ew!" she screamed as she looked up at me. I looked at her without a word. She ran away.

The television began playing the unmistakable overprocessed jangling guitar notes that foretold the introduction of yet another Mexican soap opera. A door to my right opened, and the sound of a freshly flushed toilet could be heard beyond its threshold. Short bursts of vulgarity began ringing through the windows, then very loudly through the waiting room, as two police officers half escorted, half carried an incredibly argumentative drunk man who was bleeding from the forehead. Without a single word, the officers walked him past the waiting room and down to the welcoming arms of the auxiliary police precinct inside the hospital, as their brothers in blue had done for the previous four individuals who'd found themselves in similar situations that evening.

The baby kept yelling.

Another ambulance pulled up to the dock, sirens blaring and engine roaring. The clack of a stretcher slamming against the double doors at the reception area echoed through the waiting room. The children running rampant began yelling for their parents to look at the damaged and bloodied person wheeling at high speed through the hallways leading to where I longed to be. I couldn't help thinking that, even though his wounds were far graver than my own, he was the lucky one.

This was all my fault.

Mike had been trying to make this the first birthday in many years that was actually fun. I'd been hiding out all day, and just when it looked like the day might pass with no altercations or injury, he took up his black marker. In all fairness, I really should have been paying attention to where I was putting my hand when I began stumbling backward. My Sharpie hand was poised for a strike; all I needed was a quick push from my free hand to stop my backward momentum and mount a suitable riposte. I didn't realize that, while screwing around in a fit of boredom, I'd left an uncapped X-Acto knife sitting base-down in a lump of sculpting clay.

I closed my eyes once again and let my head drop back in utter defeat. I rolled my face to the right and opened my eyes to find Mike looking at me with a mixture of pity and agony. He looked at the floor, sighed, and then looked over at me.

"Dude . . . I'm really—" he began.

"I know, man. I know," I said with yet another sigh, this one carrying with it the weight of my twenty-three previous birthdays. We both returned our gaze to the floor and resumed waiting.

I had just turned fourteen, and through what felt like a long and deep tunnel, I could hear my mother yelling at me. "For the last time, Joe," she was snarling through gritted teeth, "get out of that bed! We're not going to have your birthday party tonight if you don't go to school today!"

"Murhhnnnnhhh."

"Oh, knock it off!" she snapped, halting her exit from my room and spinning on her heel to face the lump of me lying on the bed. "You're lucky your father and I let you get away with this charade for this long. You're going to school today!"

"Gnnnnnhurrrrrrrr . . ." I muttered through my pillow, adding for emphasis a strong "Blgnnnfunf."

She placed her hands on her hips in a well-rehearsed motion. With a sigh, she said, "This is useless. I know that report cards for the midterm came out this week, and I know that you're probably failing, as usual. And I know that you will pull your grades up by the end of the semester, as always, and I know that you think this is all one big game. But you're still going to have to face your father over this report card at some point, so you might as well get up and get it over with as quickly as possib—"

I interrupted her with an incredibly powerful bout of deep chest coughing.

My poor mother stood there, torn. The noises she'd just heard rumble and flop out of her son sounded quite legitimate, indicating that perhaps *this* time he wasn't faking being sick to lay out of school. Still, there had been many previous occasions when this trick had been pulled, and in all occurrences, the sounds that I'd produced to convince my mother I was sick had become more and more authentic through constant practice. She probably thought at this point that it wasn't beneath me to go inhale chalk dust simply to produce an authentic cough. But there was one sure way to find out.

"Okay, fine!" she said, throwing up her hands. "You asked for it. We are going to the doctor today! There, how do you like *that*?"

"Phlaagggggmmmmmurrrrr . . ."

She shook her head and closed her eyes. Was I calling her bluff, trying to get her to back down by pretending I was okay with the idea, thus proving I was sick and making a trip to the doctor futile? Or was I sick and unable to put up any sort of fight? I was an awfully good bluffer, but I also hated the doctor.

"Get dressed," she said, letting her hands flop downward with resignation. "We're going to see Dr. Clopton."

I didn't move.

"Joe," she said sharply, "I told you to get dressed! That means get your butt up out of that bed and . . ."

I shifted slightly.

"I'm not kidding! Get out of that bed, or so help me . . . I'm calling your father! He wanted me to handle this, but he told me to call him if you wouldn't play ball."

I shifted again.

"RIGHT NOW, YOUNG MAN!" she snapped.

I wriggled a bit, then lifted the covers and began to roll out of bed. Literally. With a resounding thud, I hit the floor.

My poor mother. What must have been going through her head at that moment? If I was really sick, she now had to lift my 220-pound frame off that floor all by herself. But if I was faking, she'd be falling for yet more of my bluff.

She bit her bottom lip. "Okay, wise guy! You want to play it that way? FINE! I'm calling 911!" She marched out of the room, certain this would do it. I'm sure she believed I'd come jogging into the dining room midcall and put a stop to the charade. When I didn't do that, she was absolutely convinced that I'd beg her to call the 911 operator and say it was all a mistake and they should call the cavalry back. When the paramedics and police arrived, she was willing to bet the house and both of the mortgages that I would sit up, smile, and turn beet red, embarrassed beyond belief that my mother had gotten up the gall to teach me a lesson. When the ambulance came and I put up no resistance whatsoever as they carried me on a backboard out of the house, her fury grew to near-infinite proportions. Surely I couldn't be this committed to faking my illness. But after all of the bluff-calling and check-raising and going all in, it took only two words for her to lose all her chips.

"I said 'double pneumonia,'" the doctor repeated.

My mother stood there, flabbergasted. "What?" she said again.

The doctor sighed. "Mrs. Peacock, your son is *very* ill," he said, repeating his previous three sentences in yet another slightly different way. "He's got double pneumonia, bronchitis, infections in both ears, a sinus infection, he's severely dehydrated, and—"

"He's . . . he's really . . ." she stammered. She narrowed her eyes, placed her hands on her hips with that practiced motion, and stared the doctor down. "Are you *certain* that he's really sick?"

"Ma'am," the doctor said with a shocked chuckle, "I can hear all sorts of buildup in his lungs when he breathes, he's running a temperature of a hundred and two, and he's barely able to open his eyes. If he's not sick, then I need to stop practicing medicine."

My mother's face resembled a film transition as it wiped from angry to extremely sad and concerned. She began to cry. "Oh my God. He's really sick!"

The doctor looked at her for a moment. "Yes, ma'am, that's what I've been— Wait, you mean you didn't know he was sick?"

"No! Well, wait. I knew he *said* he was sick," she responded. "I mean . . . It's report card week, and he's going to lose his Nintendo, and . . ." She adopted a pleading tone. "Oh, Doctor . . . You have no idea! I mean, I know it sounds so bad, but . . . But you just don't know him!"

"You thought he was faking?"

"Well, I'M not a doctor!" she said defensively. "I don't know what real bronchitis sounds or looks like! He can fake sick really well. I mean, you just don't know my son!"

"Did it ever occur to you to take his temperature?" the doctor asked.

"It's useless!" she said. "He knows every trick in the book! He'll hold the thermometer to a lightbulb if you're not in the room, and if you are, he'll pretend he can't hold it in his mouth . . . He'll hold hot coffee in his mouth to throw it off. Doctor, seriously! You just don't know him!"

The doctor regarded this poor woman who had the son with the penchant for dodging school. "And the cough?"

"I'd just thought he'd finally perfected the sound."

"Didn't you notice he wasn't eating?"

"He has a fridge in his room," she said in a monotone, staring off into space as her mind danced around how it could be that she could miss all these signs.

"I see. Makes a habit of hibernating, does he?" he asked as he stood and went over to a small intercom.

"Yeah. He'll draw in his room for days, or read comics, or . . . OH MY GOD . . ." She began sobbing.

He finished paging a nurse to the room, then turned to comfort my poor, distraught mother. "It's all right, Mrs. Peacock," he said. "He's going to be okay."

"I'm a terrible mother!" she wailed.

"You're probably a fine mother," he said as the guilt overcame her. "I'm sure he is quite a handful, if he's as much of a devil as you say."

She kept sobbing as the nurse arrived. The doctor ordered an IV and began rattling off all sorts of multisyllabic words. My mother interrupted his orders to ask, "He needs an IV?"

"Yes," the doctor replied. "He's going to have to stay here overnight, maybe even a few days. We're going to have to get some fluids—"

My poor, poor mother just stood there and cried.

"It's . . . It's going to be all right, Mrs. Peacock . . ."

She got up and walked over to the bed. "I am so sorry," she said, taking my hand. I'm sure the sight of me in a hospital on my birthday brought back any number of bad memories.

I spent that night and much of the next day in the closest thing to a coma one can be without being in a coma. I'm not sure there's a medical term for it outside of saying that I was really, really tired from being really, really sick. But that's what I was, and that's how it went.

When I was released, I came home to a fairly nice party with a few family members in attendance (my eighth-grade year hadn't produced any real friends I'd associate with outside of school). I got a yellow Sports Walkman and a Teenage Mutant Ninja Turtles game for Nintendo, as well as some comic books I'd been asking for. And I had it all taken away, along with the Nintendo, my television privileges, my stereo, and my bike when my report card came back with five F's and an A in physical education.

Not to worry, though. I got straight B's at the end of the semester, just like I always did.

I'd long since learned how to count by the day I turned eighteen years old. But for whatever reason, the doctors wanted to test my ability to do it that day, and I'm never one to disappoint a crowd. "Ten . . ." I said slowly and deliberately. I'd been told to count backward from ten, and I'd been told to do it slowly. I hadn't been told to do it deliberately; I'd added that little bit myself because I try to go above and beyond.

"Good," the man in the green mask and green skull-cap said as he hovered over me. I didn't quite understand why he was congratulating me. I'd only just started. It's not like you can really gauge someone's overall performance based on a single digit. So I had to give him more to work with.

"Nine," I felt myself saying aloud. See? Two digits in a row, said slowly and with extra care. I could feel some movement taking place near my midsection as the man came in close, then closer, then very close to my face and examined me through safety glasses.

He looked up at a colleague. "Flibberty gibbit!" the green-masked guy said. I'm sure he didn't really say "flibberty gibbit." He probably said something else, but it came out as gibberish to me. I'm overdubbing for you, like in those Hong Kong movies you download over BitTorrent with the fan-made speech track.

"Keep going," he said to me.

"Eight," I replied. I suddenly noticed that the green-masked man was wearing paisley, which he hadn't been wearing before. Strange. But paisley flattered him. And he wasn't really wearing it; it was floating in front of him, kind of hovering on him. I could feel more movement near my midsection. A cold feeling settled on my left thigh. "Gobbledy poppycock," the man said in other words that I'm overdubbing for you, followed by even more gibberish—and gibberish on top of that.

He didn't tell me to keep going, but I decided to keep the tradition alive and say aloud the number seven. It sounded strange as I said it, as if it echoed, but without losing any volume. And it wasn't exactly an echo. It was more like a chorus.

"I was just made by the Presbyterian church," the man with the green mask said. Or maybe he didn't. Maybe I'm just really bad at subtitling. I must be from Singapore. It doesn't really matter, does it?

I could feel the cold thing on my leg. "Six."

"Klee mungle flubberduck," the knee-cutting masked guy didn't even come close to saying.

"Five." I'm only at five, I thought. I can't go any faster with the counting, okay? You're going to have to wait for me to finish before you do what you're doing there, on my leg with the cold thing, because I can feel it. I can feel it.

Okay, I can totally feel that, too. Right there, that! It's cold and it's wet and it's my knee and you're cutting into it and I know that's why I'm here and all, but really, I'm not done counting and you can't do that yet. You can't do that . . . THAT . . . OH, GOD. Gross. This is so gross. It doesn't hurt . . . Why doesn't it hurt? I can feel it. It doesn't hurt. That's . . . so weird! I can feel it and it doesn't hurt. Man, if I could do that with everything, I could be the best wrestler ever. I wouldn't have had to stop the match last year in the finals. I could have won state. Gone four years straight as the champion.

Okay, stop it, I can feel that oh my dear God.

And so it went for three straight hours. A nervous just-turned-eighteen-year-old mind racing through not enough anesthesia during a follow-up surgery on his birthday to remove the rest of a torn piece of cartilage from his left knee. It was the strangest sensation I'd ever felt in my life, and I can say with all honesty that it still is.

I can't remember the moment-by-moment experiences. It's as if every single one of them happened all at once, and my mind has put them into some sort of order based on how logic would dictate that they happened. Every scrape of the scalpel against bone, every tug of a ligament, every push and poke and application of pressure. It was like some-one pushing on me through the cushions of a couch.

Awareness and wakefulness are two different things, and even though I was out, I was still aware. My mind couldn't process everything the way it normally would, but the one thing it could figure out was that at the end of it all, I was very upset. Not because it hurt—it really didn't. It was be-cause it seemed to take forever, and I found it agonizing to try and reconcile the feelings I was experiencing. And when I "awoke," I was just cognizant enough to want to let every-one know that I was a bit upset, and just hazy enough to lack any self-control.

I felt my eyes blink. I felt hyperaware, like Daredevil. I could hear the air coming through the vent above me and to my left. I could hear the breathing of one, two, three . . . three people in the room. Each and every air molecule bounced off my tingling skin like marbles on a snare drum. I could feel each point on my body that rested on the plastic-covered foam mattress of the hospital bed.

"There he is," I heard my father say from above me. Every word was clear, almost as if they were being played through an incredibly high-fidelity speaker. I felt him stand up. I tried to turn my head to face him. I felt my left hand move. I tried to turn my head again. My right arm twitched.

"Oh, my poor baby," my mother said a bit farther to my left as she stood to come near me.

"He's going to be a bit hazy for a while," the one strange voice said from above and behind me. I knew the voice. It had congratulated me on my ability to say the word "ten." It had sat behind a mask when last I heard it.

I tried to turn to face it. I could feel my butt clench. I tried again. My left hand moved again. "Ohhhhh . . ." I said, writhing around.

"Can I help him up?" my father asked. My mother stood beside him.

"Go ahead, he should be able to sit up," the doctor said.

I felt fingers sliding under my right shoulder blade and then my left. I felt pressure pushing my back upward. I felt as though I needed to engage some sort of muscle function to assist, so I flexed my whole body. Somehow I ended up upright. I shook my head, and my eyelids shot wide open. I scanned the room. I saw posters and charts illustrating the internals of my knee.

"How are you feeling?" the masked man asked from behind me.

"Um . . . uhh . . ." I said, mentally flipping through my Rolodex of words in order to find at least two to string together that would form some sort of answer.

"Oh, you poor thing," my mother said, placing her hand

on my left shoulder. My father left his hand on my right shoulder, holding me steady. "You poor, poor thing . . ."

"And you said it'll be two or three weeks before he's up and around on it?" my father asked, clearly picking up from a previous conversation.

"Yeah," the surgeon said, "I don't think it'll be much longer than that. This was just a clean-up job. He should be fully functional in a few weeks."

"He's going to be able to wrestle on it?" my father said. "He was out for months after the last one." I wobbled a little. My father steadied me.

"I think so, with enough care and a little physical therapy," the surgeon said, walking around from behind me. "Because he didn't sustain any injury to the area this time, there's not really much recovery taking place. He needs to heal up at the incision site, which will be plenty enough time for the site of the removed meniscus to get healed up. He'll be good to go for the state tournament, I'm pretty sure."

"But he's going to miss the Southside Classic," my mother stated plainly.

"He should be fine for that," my dad said, "if it only takes—"

"He's *not* going to be in it," my mother stated again.

"Oh, I dunno," the surgeon said, coming closer. "That's in March as well, isn't it? He should be all right."

"I really think that's a bad idea," my mother said.

"Well, it's going to be up to him," the surgeon said. "He's pretty strong. Very resilient. Besides, he'll want the practice. Won't you, champ?" He reached out, and my father removed his hand so the surgeon could male-bond with me and give me a pat on the shoulder.

It was so cold. I could feel the whole room and the volume that each object took up; the air moving in and out of everyone's lungs. I could feel myself looking down at the surgeon's hand on my right shoulder. I could feel my left shoulder tense. I could feel my elbow push backward, and my fingers wrapping tightly into my palm, and my thumb wrapping over the top of my fingers . . . I could feel myself looking up at him. My eyelids popped wide open and I felt the air hitting my eyeballs. I could feel the skin of my forearm wrinkle slightly as it whipped backward, and I could feel it change direction as it flung straight ahead. I could feel myself lurching forward.

I felt his jaw buckle under my fist.

I could feel myself falling. I could feel him falling. I could feel my father pulling my groggy body up off the ground. And that was when, of all the times that day I could have possibly done it, I passed out completely.

Was he upset? Well, sorta. He didn't have me arrested or anything, but I was restrained and then escorted off the premises that day. It took a few years, but the surgeon eventually accepted my apology when he ended up having to fill in for my regular orthopedic for a routine scoping of my knee. He never got the full story until that day, and once I told him what had happened, he understood completely. But he wasn't too pleased when I told him "Mega googly zapperdap." Or maybe I just called him a cocksucker. I can't be sure. Like I said, I suck at subtitles.

It was my fifteenth birthday, and by all accounts, it should have been the best day of my entire life.

Since it had been released the previous fall, all I'd wanted in the world was a Super Nintendo entertainment system (SNES). It was the ultimate in video-gaming badassery. Every single commercial depicting happy children playing *Super Mario World* had played in my head just about every waking moment of my life since I'd heard the jingle "Now you're playing with power . . . SUPER power!"

And when I got a SNES for my birthday, I thought that the world was going to crack in half from the sheer power of my enthusiasm. It was the last thing on earth I'd expected, due to the fact that my family was going through extremely tough financial times. But my father, being the hero of a man he was, knew how much it would mean to me to have one—and how much motivation it would give me to keep my grades up in school. After all, the last thing a fifteen-year-old boy wanted was for the entire meaning of his existence to be snatched from him and placed in his parents' closet because he'd gotten a D in English.

It was manners that held me at the dining room table until all of the visiting family members had left that afternoon. It would have been rude to open the SNES, yell "HAHAHAHAHA I GOT IT FUCK ALL Y'ALL," and leave to play it until my eyes bled. I probably would have had it taken away before I'd even gotten the power supply connected. But as they all stood up and indicated their intentions to leave, I couldn't help but wish them a fond farewell as many times in as short a time frame as possible as would convince them to get the hell out of my house and leave me to my sixteen-bit goodness.

When it was announced that my seventeen-year-old cousin Stevie wanted to stay the night, I thought, Good—someone else to play with! Stevie had an SNES—he'd gotten one the day it came out, just like everything else on the planet that he ever wanted. So of course, I thought, he should be pretty good at *Super Mario World*. Maybe he could teach me some secrets or show me a code or some sort of insider information gained by being one of the first people to own everything.

But no. Stevie didn't have any insider information. He didn't possess any codes. In fact, he confessed that he hadn't even played *Super Mario World* since the second day after he'd gotten his SNES. He didn't want to explore Vanilla Dome or the Forest of Illusion. He couldn't care less about discovering the secrets of Star Road, and he didn't want to visit Yoshi's House. No, Stevie wanted to go to Catherine's house.

"Catherine?" I asked. "As in Catherine Swinger?"

"Yeah," he said.

"As in Swinger the Swinger, Catherine Swinger?"

"Yeah," he said again, this time with a smile.

"Uh, no, thanks," I said, plopping down on the bed and pulling on the tabs on the side of the box that held my Super Nintendo.

"Come *on*, dude," my cousin demanded. "Do you know how bad this chick wants me?"

I winced at the very thought. I barely knew Catherine

from seeing her around the halls of my school—she was a junior and I a freshman. Still, having inhabited the locker rooms of both the football and wrestling teams that year, I'd heard her name more than once, and from what little I knew of her, she was quite popular with the boys. And not particularly due to her looks (which, from what I'd seen, would scare the paint off walls). But she put out, and that's quite a redeeming quality for the socially climbing high school girl. For Stevie, the thought of sexual conquest outside the confines of his own school's echoing halls was too strong to resist.

"Stevie, I don't *care* how bad she wants you," I answered. "It's my birthday, I just got a Super Nintendo, and I want to stay here and play it. You can go if you want, but I'm staying right here."

"Duuuuuuude . . ." he said, clenching his fists and stomping a bit. "You have to come with me. I don't know where she lives!"

"Call her, then!" I said. "She can give you directions. Hell, I'll draw you a map!"

"Dammit," he said, "you won't do this? Not for me?"

"No," I answered. "I don't like Catherine. I don't like any of her friends, and I don't like the idea of having to deal with the whispers and jeers that are going to come when people find out that my cousin ended up sleeping with her."

"Why not?" he asked. "What the hell do you care what people say about me?"

"Because," I said, pulling a controller from the plastic wrap, "all anyone is going to hear are the words 'Peacock,' 'fucked,' and 'Catherine.' They'll draw their own conclusions. I don't need that."

"Heh." He chuckled. "That just might be the best thing for you."

"Yeah, well," I said, flipping the plug of the controller around to figure out how the holes lined up with the slot on the console, "I'm happy where I stand on the social map for now."

"Nobody knows who you are," he said. "You said so yourself."

When I was ten years old, my mother married my father (who adopted me when I was fourteen). This not only made Stevie my cousin, it also moved me from inner-city Atlanta, Georgia, to super-suburban Jonesboro. I ended up in a situation where everyone knew everyone else, and I was the odd fat kid out (it also didn't help that I was the only white kid listening to Eric B. & Rakim at the time). Junior high was equally hellish, because everyone was in the same districts. It was pure luck that they'd redrawn the lines my freshman year of high school, sending me to Mount Zion High School and everyone else to Jonesboro High. I adored the change. For the first time since I'd moved to that city, I was completely free to be known for who I was and not who I had been as a child.

It was with that thought in mind that I snapped, "Yeah, and that's precisely how I like it."

"Whatever, dude!" Stevie whined. "I can't believe you won't help your cousin out here!"

"I can't believe you're asking me to go sit in some girl's house while you bang her in the bedroom," I replied. "Especially when I just got a freakin' SNES!"

"Come on," he said, relying on his standard argument. Stevie was quite a handsome young man. He wasn't too short or too tall, sitting right at the five-feet-ten mark. He had sandy blond hair, bright blue eyes, and a smile that had apparently been getting him laid since he was twelve. He had a confidence that seemed neither bold nor overbearing; he had a natural understanding that what he wanted, he could get.

It pretty much always worked on everyone he knew except me. I was oblivious to subtlety or the wily charms of cute boys. I hated cute boys. In fact, I despised them. I wanted to punch them and throw them through walls, for it had been cute boys who'd made my life hell throughout my early school life. Stevie was the only exception to this rule—I'd always liked him, even though he shared the traits of my tormentors. But the natural consequence of having such a dire prejudice against pretty people was that I was immune to the poisons of their charm.

"Fine," Stevie said with a small pout. "If you don't go, I'm telling your mom and dad about your porn stash."

I threw down the controller, stood up from the edge of my bed, and walked over to him. I looked into his eyes, his growing smirk visible in the periphery of my vision. Given the recent excitement that had resulted from my mother finding my first ever pornographic acquisition, Stevie clearly knew exactly where to hit me to make me hurt the most.

"Fine. Let's go."

The walk to Catherine's house was uneventful, unless you count my not saying a single word to Stevie as an event. She lived a few blocks over from where I lived—just close enough to be on my school bus route and just far enough to maintain an uncomfortable level of silence with a horny cousin intent on adding another notch to his belt. When we got there, I stood on the stoop with my hands in my jacket pockets and my face in a scowl as Stevie knocked on the door.

"Hey, baby," Catherine said as the door creaked open. "Good to see you again!"

"Thanks," I said. "Wish I felt the same."

She sneered as she looked me up and down. "Not you. I don't even know you."

"Yeah, you do," I said. "I'm the cousin of the guy you've met once and are about to share your pubic lice with."

"Fuck you," she said.

I smirked and looked at Stevie. "Now I think she's talking to you."

Stevie smirked back at me. He and I were as opposite as opposite could be. But we were family, and we loved each other. Because of that, he could still find the humor in my game-killing. He smiled, slapped my left arm with the back of his right hand, and nodded toward the door. We both entered.

He and Catherine started going at it pretty much right away—no small talk, no emotional buildup. I supposed they'd done enough talking over the phone the past few weeks. They'd met at one of my wrestling matches in December, and according to Stevie, they'd been sharing fairly hot talk since. Maybe they'd gotten all of that out of the way earlier. Either that or both my cousin and Catherine were big, big whores.

"Hey," I heard Catherine say to me from somewhere inside Stevie's mouth, "keep an eye out. If my family comes home, give us a heads-up, will you?"

"I'm sure you'll be getting enough of a heads-up as it is," I replied.

Catherine snorted. "C'mon," Stevie said as he looked over at me. "You got my back, right?"

I smirked. "Yeah, man, I'll keep an eye out."

The pair descended into the bowels of her bedroom, so I went ahead and made myself comfortable on the living room couch. I was scanning the room, passing judgment on the family with each picture frame, figurine, and yard-sale art piece my eyes took in. As I evaluated their television, the concept of possibly making the time go by a little faster made itself apparent, and I began looking for the remote. It wasn't on the coffee table, and it wasn't on the sofa. I didn't see it on the chair or the love seat.

Great, I thought. This is one of those families who puts away the remote every time they're done watching TV. I bet they live in denial of how much television they watch, telling all of their friends that they catch only one or two shows a week, and they rarely let the kids watch it. I bet they get a huge thrill out of how impressed their friends must be with how contemporary and elite they are, and all the while they're watching the hell out of some *Letterman*. I bet they also didn't know that their daughter was a big ugly slut.

I stood up and uncomfortably began opening drawers and cabinet doors on the entertainment center, when lo and behold, I saw a fully armed and operational Super Nintendo sitting there, just begging me to play it. And since it was my birthday, and since I'd been so unjustly ripped away from my own SNES . . .

It took me all of five seconds to get everything turned on and plop my ass on the couch with controller in hand. In under a minute, I was inside Yoshi's House, learning about how the princess had been kidnapped and whatnot. Before I knew it, I was exploring the Vanilla Dome, much like Catherine was doing with my cousin.

I'd read in last month's *Nintendo Power* about some secret exits from the various stages. If you could find a key item and carry it to the proper point, you could unlock a hidden exit and make your way up the mythical and all-powerful Star Road. It didn't matter that I didn't get to explore this secret on my own SNES . . . as long as I got to explore it. Soon enough, I found the secret exit from Ghost House #1—the one that unlocked the unlimited 1-UP block and all the super flowers and feathers I could get my hands on. I was giddy as hell: ninety-nine lives, here I come! This knowledge was going to make getting to Star Road so much easier.

I was somewhere around 1-UP number sixty-three when I heard a small clicking sound. At first it didn't quite register to me as a small clicking sound. It registered as one of those events in life that simply does not matter one bit because you're playing Super Nintendo and you're getting massive 1-UPs and holy shit, it's so awesome. But then the clicking sound turned into a clacking sound, and as we all know, whenever you hear a click followed by a clack, there are only a few things it could be. Once I heard another click after the clack, and then a creak, I knew it was time to panic.

So panic I did. I stood bolt upright. I dropped the controller, and I fled down the hallway off the living room. I heard a small din of conversation from the area of the door, and many small moaning sounds coming from the end of the hallway. My first instinct was to leap out the first window I found, saving my own skin and letting Stevie get what was coming to him. But like I said: We're family.

I ran down the hallway, following the moaning sounds to the last bedroom on the right. I tried the door—it was locked. The door noises silenced the moaning, and I heard someone whisper something ever so lightly, something that sounded like "What was that?" I then heard major rustling and commotion as I tried the doorknob again.

The laughter and conversation grew louder in the hallway as Catherine's family entered the living room. I could hear Yoshi's Theme playing from the speakers on the television as someone questioned why the Super Nintendo was on.

I tried the doorknob again. More rustling. A few stomps and some banging around. Louder talk from the living room.

I tried the door again. This time it swung open, revealing Catherine in a hastily applied sweatshirt with extremely mussed hair. She looked frantic and embarrassed and completely shocked to see me standing there. Her shock then relaxed into annoyance. "Oh. You," she said.

"Your family just got home!" I whispered, adding a slight nod down the hallway toward the living room.

The shock and embarrassment immediately returned.

She grabbed my arm and pulled me into the room, closing the door behind her.

"Where is Steven?" I asked in hushed tones, scanning the room.

She pointed toward an open window as her answer. "Go!" she whispered.

Just then a knock came at the door.

"Cathy?" a male voice said. "You okay, darlin'?"

Catherine and I looked at each other. Panicked, we redoubled our efforts to get me the fuck out of there. "I'm . . . I'm fine, Daddy!" she said.

"You sure, honey?" The doorknob clicked slightly, as if being opened slowly and with great concern for the privacy of person on the other side . . . but not enough concern to stay out.

She ushered me through the window. "I'm okay, Daddy, I swear!" she bellowed. I examined it—the screen had been bent up, obviously due to the fact that neither of the two people attempting to gain access to the outdoors knew how to undo the clips at the top of the window. I noticed that the clips on the bottom had been bent off and broken.

The doorknob stalled after a certain point, prompting the person turning it to try turning it again. "Is this door locked?" her father asked. "Why is this door locked?"

"Daddy, I'm . . . I'm getting *dressed*!" she yelled. I stepped through the window with my right leg and lifted the bent portion of the screen as much as I could so I could bring my body through. I was just crossing the threshold when my left pants leg became snagged on one of the broken clips.

I attempted to lift my leg up and off the clip while balancing on my right toe. I was nearly off when I heard a shrill scream, followed by "Oh my God, WHO ARE YOU?"

This is where it got ugly. Catherine's mother, having forgotten something in the car and heading back out to get it, found me climbing out of her daughter's window. She shrieked, then ran inside to fetch Catherine's father. I desperately began tugging and yanking at my pants leg to get it to come loose, all the while embedding the snag deeper and deeper. Catherine pressed on my left foot with all her might while I pulled on my leg, which—with a loud ripping sound—at last freed me from the skank's window.

I tumbled to the grass right beneath Catherine's window. A bit confused and a lot panicked, I'd begun picking myself up off the ground when I heard a sharp "Psssst!" coming from someplace close by. I looked around, unable to find the source of the noise, when I heard it again.

"Psssst!" said one of the bushes in the neighbor's yard. "Over here!"

"Stevie?" I asked as I stumbled over to it.

"Shhhhh!" he said as I came alongside the large shrub where he'd found concealment. There was some yelling from directly across, inside Catherine's room. It was followed by some shouting, then some outright screaming. "We gotta get out of here," Stevie whispered.

"Okay, then, let's go," I said, and turned to leave.

"We can't just walk down the road!"

"Why not?" I said. "We gotta go, don't we?"

"Yeah, but they'll see us!"

"So?" I answered. "They don't know who we are. They

didn't see us come in, right? All they saw was a foot hanging out of a window. They could hardly identify a foot."

Stevie thought for a second.

"They have no idea it was you banging their daughter, right?" I asked.

Stevie thought some more.

"If we just walk down the road, all normal-like, we'll look like neighborhood kids out for a walk, right?"

Stevie considered this impeccable piece of wisdom and then agreed. "Okay, let's move."

The plan was solid. The plan was great. The plan combined common sense with situational awareness and provided us a perfectly executed exit strategy. What the plan did not take into consideration was the fact that we had to cross the yard to get to the road. And normal neighborhood kids, out for a normal neighborhood walk, rarely traipsed through the backyard of someone whose daughter had just been pilfered. A fact that Catherine's rifle-wielding father had clearly considered as he burst through the front door of the house and shouted, "STOP RIGHT THERE!"

We stopped right there. In fact, we stopped right there so fast and so well that we should have won an award.

"Back in the house!" he barked from the porch. I would have complied right then, but the shock of experiencing, for the first time, someone pulling a gun on me, after I'd escaped through his daughter's window, for playing their SNES while my cousin banged her—it certainly gave me pause. Apparently Stevie as well, because we both stood there not moving a muscle.

"NOW!"

We did what any sensible teenagers would do when faced with this situation. We ran. It took about three steps for me to reach full speed, and when I did, I broke all land speed records held currently by any man or machine. My breathing was deep and rushed, and my feet slapped loudly against the asphalt as my torn pants leg flapped in the rush of wind created by churning legs. I could hear Stevie keeping pace beside me. From somewhere behind us, I heard Catherine's father yelling something; I couldn't tell what it was. I just knew that he was yelling. But the next sound was unmistakable.

The report of a rifle shot echoed through the air.

After that, I didn't hear my feet pounding the pavement, I didn't hear Stevie beside me, I didn't hear shit besides my heart pounding in my ears, my face, my legs, my chest. It was like going deaf except for one sound that shook you to your core.

We ran. We ran until the rubber melted off our sneakers and our blood became carbonated with the amount of air our lungs pushed into it. And when we finally got home, we kept on running. We ran through the front door; we ran down the hall. We ran into my bedroom. If it were possible to run into a chair while sitting in it, we did that, too.

"Holy . . ." I said, gasping for air.

"Dude . . ." Steven said, lifting a limp finger that swayed up and down with each desperate breath he took.

I thought he was trying to give me a high five. I didn't want to give him a high five. I couldn't even bear the thought of giving him a high five after what he'd put me through. But I was too busy to curse at him and dismissively wave away his feeble high five, so I closed my eyes and continued huffing and puffing.

"Joe," he said, finger still extended.

"Go . . . Go fuck . . ." I said through breaths, trying to tell him what he could with his spare index finger.

"Look," he said, his arm still extended, his hand still bobbing, his body still heaving with the gasping for air.

I looked at his arm. I visually traced his bicep as it led to his forearm, which held out the limp wrist and even limper index finger. I drew an imaginary line from the tip of his finger outward and followed it to my left leg, which was leaking blood from the calf in rather large amounts. The ripped remains of my pants leg were damp and purple with my blood. My sock glowed a bright crimson. My sneakers looked like they'd been designed by some first-year fashion design student with a pirated version of Adobe Photoshop.

"Oh, shit," I said. I'd been exasperated only a moment before, but suddenly, my body no longer craved oxygen. I was completely unable to breathe. The beating of my heart in my ears gave way to a loud ringing, and the world swirled and went black as I fell over in a slump.

When I awoke, I discovered that quite a lot had transpired during my little siesta. Stevie told my parents that I'd been shot in the leg (after all, there was a gunshot, and I was bleeding profusely from the leg). And when they asked very frantically why anyone would do such a thing, he merely indicated that a crazy man had fired his rifle from his porch while we were running down the street.

My mother took me to the emergency room, and my father went over to Catherine's house and introduced himself to her father. Within seconds, according to Stevie, my dad had the man by the throat and barely touching the ground with his tiptoes. He interrogated Catherine's father, demanding to know why he'd felt it necessary to discharge a firearm into his son's leg.

Catherine's father replied with a series of gurgles and spurts that, while probably satisfying to hear, didn't really answer my father's question. So he tossed the man around the room a bit and asked again. Catherine's father replied that he'd pointed the rifle straight into the sky and fired into the air, simply to scare us, so there was no way my wound could have come from that. He then proceeded to elaborate on Stevie's version of the story, shedding a bit more light on why he might have felt the need to fire a gun in the air to scare us and where the wound on my left leg had come from. He went so far as to give my father the nickel tour of the house, showing him the SNES controller that I'd played with and the room where Catherine had wiggled Stevie's joystick. Catherine's father even showed my father the chunk of metal from the ripped and folded screen, complete with tiny chunks of denim and leg meat. It was clear that I had not been shot but, instead, had had my leg torn open by a hastily opened screen hook.

In light of this new evidence, my father apologized and instantly turned the full brunt of his anger and aggravation on me. This resulted in my parents returning the SNES that they'd bought me for my birthday. They said it was to teach me a lesson about peer pressure and about taking responsibility for my actions. They told me that I never should have agreed to go over there, and barring that, when the family got home, I shouldn't have run like a coward.

I know that it's because the deductible for the hospital visit was about the same cost as the SNES, and they couldn't afford both. But I definitely admire the way they spun it to add morals and whatnot.

"Fuck you! I ain't coming out!" I screamed with my little infant mouth from the other side of my mother's belly. "Put all the drops you want in her nose, you ain't gettin' me outta here!"

Well, what did you expect? It was cold the day I was born! In fact, January 24, 1977, once held the record in Georgia for the coldest day in the history of January 24ths. There was an ice storm going on, for chrissake—and I'm not sure if you remember what it's like in a womb, but if you don't, it's a heck of a lot warmer than a damn ice storm.

So I stood fast. I planted my feet, grabbed on tight, and turned blue in the face. And the arms. And the legs, chest, and every other little place that should have been bright pink. In fact, when the doctors and nurses finally got me the heck out of there, they found a thirteen-pound baby who was one white hat and a cute song away from being a Smurf.

At the time they had no idea what was wrong with me, mostly because the Internet hadn't become a widely used tool for the common human, so they couldn't visit my Web site and see how stubborn I really am. They sat there and scratched their heads and muttered a little and finally decided that, whatever was causing it, it definitely wasn't a positive thing. So they decided to just go nuts.

According to my mother, they began preparations to fly me via helicopter to Houston to the best neonatal cardiac care unit in the nation. That would have been ultracool, honestly, as I've never been in a helicopter in my life, and if they'd done that, I wouldn't be able to say that. Not only because I would have been in a helicopter but also because I most definitely would have died, since my blue hue had nothing to do with my heart.

They put both my mother and me in a screaming ambulance flying west from South DeKalb Medical Center in Decatur to Grady Memorial in Atlanta, the two of us surrounded by twelve cardiac specialists, neonatal specialists, and assistants to the specialists. While in transit to Grady, a very sharp young doctor named Janet decided—against all conventional medical wisdom—to ask my mother a few questions.

You see, my mother had prenatal pneumonia. Because of this, her little unborn Smurf had lungs that were filled with fluid. From those rather morbid discussions that always seem to come up in high school biology involving drowning and suffocation, we all know that when the lungs can't get oxygen, the blood can't get oxygen, and when the blood has no oxygen, it turns blue.

So we arrived at Grady with a whole new course of action—get the Smurf into the neonatal intensive care unit (NICU). Only, there was trouble at the door. You see, I come from a very long line of smart-asses. My mother?

She's a smart-ass. And her father? Yep: a smart-ass. There had obviously been some argument over what this new addition to the family was going to be named.

My mother really liked William Joseph as a name. My birth father wanted me to be a "junior" (which baffles me, given that he didn't even like me all that much), so he was pushing for Randal Joseph, Jr. My grandfather, he didn't like any of it except for Joseph. So, while my mother and birth father gave my name as William Joseph at South DeKalb, my grandfather—who sped over to Grady to jump-start the check-in process—checked me in as Haud Nom Bar Joseph.

Which, in Hebrew, apparently means No Name But Joseph.

Great, Granddad. Name your grandson Anonymous. That's freakin' brilliant. It helped when they were trying to label the charts, and it really made getting me through the door super-simple.

The doctors rushed this anonymous Smurf down a hallway while taking my poor mother into another room. She had no idea that, while he was being wheeled down the hallway en route to the NICU, her brand-new baby's brand-new heart stopped making brand-new beats.

And there you go. Inside of an hour of being born, this Peacock was no more.

They revived me and stuck me in a room that would end up costing my parents somewhere in the neighborhood of twenty-five thousand dollars a day to house me (I was pretty young, so I don't remember what the strippers looked like or what brand of champagne they served in that room).

It was about four days of intensive care later before my mom could even come in and see me—during which time my heart managed to stop beating four more times. When she was finally able to see me, she had to put her hands in these huge robot-looking gloves to pick me up.

When she did, she somehow ripped the IV out of my head, causing a small dent and a bald spot on my head that persists to this day (and let me tell you, the only thing more fun than going through middle school with a haircut mandated by my father that showed off my dented-in bald spot was trying to tell this story without having the other kids say, "Man, too bad you survived"). And why would I have an IV in my head? Well, they put the IV in my wrist, and in some sort of fit, I kicked it, and it pierced my skin. The puncture wound didn't simply heal up, however—it formed a small flap of skin over another layer of skin, such that there is a hole in my right wrist that served as a constant source of entertainment through my teen years when I shoved nails and body jewelry through it and freaked everyone out. So I have two everlasting scars to remind me of the first through fourth times I almost died.

If that weren't enough, after they drained my lungs, I ended up developing jaundice, turning from blue to yellow and confusing just about every LSD experimenter in the building. This caused me to move from living on a respiratory machine and a feeding tube to living under a black light for a few days. Once that was done, I developed an infection in my navel, which had to be cleaned out nearly hourly lest I become septic.

Every time they'd call my mom and say, "You can take

him home now," she'd show up to find the doctors laughing and saying, "Just kidding, he's got something else wrong with him!"

Finally, I gave up and accepted the fact that I was going to end up staying here on earth. I spent a total of fourteen days in the NICU, running up nearly three hundred and fifty thousand dollars in hospital bills (which, adjusted for inflation, ends up being nearly a million dollars).

And you thought this book was expensive.

CHAPTER 4

1-800-STALKER

"Uh, hi, guys," I said as my roommates entered the living room.

Mike and Juan stood in the entry foyer, staring at both me and the lump o' strange girl lying on the couch. As if telepathically linked, they both unleashed huge, knowing grins at me.

"No, no," I said, answering their unspoken macho congratulations. "It's not what it looks like."

"No?" Juan said as Mike carried the groceries past me and into the kitchen, smiling all the while. "It looks to me like you wore her out!"

"Uh, no," I said, standing up to help grab the Kroger bags dangling from Juan's fingers, "that wasn't me . . . that was her flight."

Mike poked his head through the doorway and into the living room. "Wait—what? Her flight?"

"Yeah," I answered. "From Phoenix."

Grins turned to gaping mouths as Juan and Mike looked

at each other and then back at me. With a sigh, I nodded Juan toward the kitchen doorway where Mike stood, indicating that there was a lot of 'splaining to do.

"Can you believe this shit?" Juan said to Mike, who was alternating glancing between Juan, me, and a jar of cookies.

"Come on, man," I said. "At least give me a chance to explain this."

"Nope," Juan responded as he walked over to the cupboard and began pulling down some form of Sara Lee snackycake.

"Why not?" I asked.

"Because you're full of shit?" he said with a teensy bit of hostility.

"What!" I shouted. "Why would I make this up?"

Juan snorted. "Let's just say that this isn't the first story of yours that I've not been able to bring myself to believe."

That much was true. What he left out—what he always leaves out—is that eventually, they all prove themselves to be true, and he always just sneers and says, "Eh, whatever," and continues to disbelieve me no matter what I tell him. Such is the way Juan is.

"I don't really care if you believe me or not," I said. "The major point here is that there is a thirty-five-year-old chick from Phoenix whom I hardly know, sleeping on our couch, and I don't know how to get rid of her."

Juan turned and looked at me. "You want her gone?" he asked.

"Well . . . yeah," I said. "She's creeping me the hell out. But how do you do that?"

He marched over to the kitchen door. "Watch," he said, just before slamming the door open. With a huge crash, the door bounced off the adjacent wall and swung back at him, forcing him to push it open far more gently to get it out of his way. "Hey!" he shouted as he approached the couch.

The sleeping crazy chick stirred slightly. "Huh?" she muttered.

Mike and I walked into the living room as Juan knelt down to get face-to-face with the nutjob. "You can't stay here," he said plainly.

"Huh?" she said, struggling to sit up and struggling even harder to open her eyes.

Juan sighed and hung his head momentarily before returning to posture. "You," he said, pointing at her. He then swung his hand toward the front door and added, "Have got to go."

"What? Why?" the chick said.

"To tell you the truth, I don't know, either," he replied. "But Joe doesn't want you here, so off you go!"

"Wow," Mike managed to squeak out.

"Wait . . . You . . . you don't want me to stay?" the crazy chick said as she looked toward me, her bedraggled hair hanging in her face.

"Well—" I said.

"Well, nothing!" Juan interjected. "You just got done telling me you don't want her here!"

"Wait," I said, attempting to do damage control on this rapidly scorching earth. "You didn't even let me tell you what was going on!"

"You didn't need to!" he said. "You said she was crazy

and you don't want her here. I told her to leave. Problem solved, right?" He headed toward the stairs. "Now come on, let's go play some *GoldenEye*."

The dazed and confused girl on our couch blinked a few times and looked at me in disbelief. "You . . . you called me crazy?"

"I, uh . . . Well, yeah, I guess I did . . ."

She sat there for a moment, absorbing the situation. "What the fuck?" she finally said, shaking her head and throwing her hands toward the sky before letting them fall in her lap. "Why did you tell me I could stay, then?"

"You don't have anywhere to go." I looked around the room for emphasis, as if staring through the walls and out into the large expanse of places just outside our house that she could not go.

"I'm not going to stay here if you don't want me to!" she shouted.

"Great!" Juan said as he began marching up the stairs. The hallway echoed with his voice as he shouted, "Come on, guys! *GoldenEye!*"

The room became uncomfortably quiet. It had been uncomfortable before, but with the quiet added on, it took on a whole new dimension. "Look, I'm . . . I'm really sorry," I tried to say, knowing I was saying it only to make myself feel better.

"You're sorry?" she blurted, brushing her hair out of her face with the back of her hand. "*You're* sorry?"

"Um . . . yes?" I said, hoping I'd chosen correctly. Mike just stood behind me, watching.

"Yeah, I bet you are," she scoffed. She tossed aside the

blanket I'd brought down for her and began looking around for her socks and shoes. "I bet you're *really* sorry that some-one has taken an interest in you! I bet you're sorry that you've got someone here who understands you . . . or at least thought she did . . ."

I sighed. "Look—"

"No, you know what? You know what? *I'm* sorry!" she yelled, pulling her left sock onto her foot. "Yeah . . . that's right, I'm the one who's sorry here! I'm sorry I fucking flew here, I'm sorry I talked to you on the phone all those nights . . ."

I began thinking back to "all those nights," and I could count a scant four nights in total. Four nights of phone-based conversation. Four nights of simply killing time. Four simple nights that, right then, I regretted ever happened. Not that they were great by any measure, I'd regretted them the moment they occurred. But being forced to go back and count them just drove home the point.

"ANSWER ME!" she screamed, jarring me out of my trance.

"And what would you have me say?" I replied, trying to play like I was in complete control when in actuality, I hadn't heard a word she'd said.

"I don't know—like 'Thank you, Jessica'? Like 'Thanks for spending all that money to come out and see me, Jessica'? You know, something like that?"

"Um . . ." I replied. "I don't think . . ."

"Yeah, you don't think, do you!" she screamed, putting her other shoe on. "You don't even think about how hard it must have been for me to step on that plane and come out here, not knowing what I was walking into. God, what an idiot I am!"

I couldn't think of anything to say. On the one hand, I really did feel bad for Jessica. I imagined the flight wasn't cheap, and I knew that she'd expended a tremendous amount of effort to get to Atlanta just to see me—a guy she'd talked to for a few weeks but somehow felt compelled to fly across the country to meet. On the other hand, she was only one shoe away from walking out the door, and I really didn't want to interrupt that.

"Whatever! *Whatever!* Just . . . ARRRGH!" she said, standing up and grabbing her bright red suitcase from beside the couch. "Just . . . don't ever call me again! Okay? Don't do it! I mean it!"

Given that the only time I'd called her had been a fluke, I didn't find that hard to agree to. "Okay," I replied with a shrug.

Her eyes popped out of her skull, and her jaw hit the floor. "'Okay'? That's all you have to say?"

"Um, yes?" I said, guessing again.

She turned in a huff, her reddish-brown hair twirling around behind her. She marched to the front door and yanked on the doorknob only to be stymied by Juan's habitual need to lock the door every single time it was closed. With a grunt, she twisted the lock one way and tried the knob, then twisted it the other way and tried again. With a strained noise, she turned the tumbler and was able to open the door.

"Just . . . FUCK YOU!" she screamed as she

pushed against the screen door and went absolutely nowhere, storming directly into it. Juan habitually locked that one as well.

I tried to hold back my laughter as she fumbled with the latch and got it open, then stomped outside, slamming the door behind her.

"Wow," Mike said. I turned to face him. He wore a gigantic grin. "So . . ."

"Don't start," I said, executing a perfect face-palm.

"Someone got a little more than he 'ordered,' I see?"

"Please, no puns."

"Did you have to press zero to let her in the house?"

Without a word, I marched into the kitchen, giving him a less than gentle shove as I passed him.

"Okay, okay! Seriously," he said, falling into step behind me, "I just have to ask one question, and it's an honest question, okay?"

I sighed. "Fine."

"So answer it honestly, okay?" he said.

"Yes, yes!" I said, grabbing a mug from the cabinet and placing it under the faucet. "Just ask the damn question."

"Why the hell is she here?"

I took a drink of water and chased it with a deep breath. "You want the whole story?"

He grabbed the jar of cookies from the counter and took a seat at the kitchen table. With a light waving gesture, he invited me to sit in my usual spot.

"Well, all right," I said as I took my seat. "And you're going to let me actually tell it?"

"Don't I always?" Mike said with a smile.

"Like I was trying to tell Juan, you know that 1-800-MUSIC-NOW thing?"

He nodded.

"Well . . ."

I was only two and a half weeks into my career as the Webmaster for BOBB Systems, and only two weeks into discovering that my job was way easier than the company thought it was.

Now, because it was 1997 and a number of people inside the company had dismissed the Internet as a "nonprofit-generating entity" or a "toy," there had been internal struggle and conflict from the first day I took the job. The only person who saw merit in the concept of putting this software company on the Internet was my boss, Gary. He was a bit of a visionary who saw the potential in hiring a dedicated resource to understand the Internet and harness its power: me.

I did a fairly good job of it, if I do say so myself. I set up a relationship between BOBB Systems—the largest ERP software developer in the world—and Monster.com, so that we received premium placement on this upstart's job-seeking Web site. I had automated scripts posting our open career positions to Usenet and funneling résumés matching certain criteria to the recruiters in our company. I set up an engine to allow marketing, HR, and legal to post all of their press releases and articles to the Web site without having to send them to me first. I also created a page on our company's Web site where the software developers could release updates to the platform that BOBB Systems wrote for the supply chain sectors.

Once my first week on the job had rolled by, I found myself in possession of about six free hours a day. This gave me two choices:

1. Go ahead and leave for the day and clue everyone in to just how little work it took to earn such a high salary, causing a huge political riot and pretty much guaranteeing that my salary—or worse, my job—would be cut, or

2. Make it look like I was working all day.

I'll leave it to you to figure out which one I chose.

Just sitting in front of a keyboard tip-tapping all day may be work in most departments, but I was under a massive amount of not undue scrutiny. I had to go the extra mile to convey my state of constant job-related panic. I couldn't simply use IRC and play *You Don't Know Jack*. I had to incorporate other means of Method acting, which was where 1-800-MUSIC-NOW came in.

This concept seems quaint nowadays, but back then, dialing a toll-free number to hear clips of music from your favorite bands and then, with the push of a button, ordering their album was quite revolutionary. I probably single-handedly funded the first two quarters of the company's revenue figures, as I spent easily three hours a day dialing in and tapping in the names of bands I figured they couldn't possibly have music for, only to be pleasantly surprised enough to push one and add that album to my basket. Not only did this build out my music collection quite handsomely, it had the double benefit of making me look like I was on the phone with the support teams of one of the three hundred or so IT vendors we did business with.

"Look, I don't care who you need to call," said Darina, one of the company's international recruiters, "I need you to handle this!"

"Sorry, I can't," I told her as I speedwalked down one of the building's main corridors. While it was elegant and quite beautiful, the building's architect must have been a fan of *The Shining,* because he'd built one of the longest damn hallways I'd ever walked through.

"But I really need those résumés!" she yelped. "Where are they?"

"I don't know," I said, lying through my teeth. From day one, Darina had been one of the biggest objectors to my position, and she wasn't at all shy about letting everyone know. As the technology recruiter who had been forced to hire me, she knew exactly how much I got paid and how old I was, and neither fact sat well with her. She took every opportunity to find ways to convince anyone who would listen that my job did not need to exist. So I found every way possible to inconvenience her. Such is the reason that the system had been dumping any and all résumés for the newly created and much needed development director position into a hidden mailbox on the server, waiting for me to find the "virus" that blocked them.

"Can't you at least *look*?" she half asked, half demanded.

"I sure can," I said, reaching the doorway to my office.

"But I've got to get on the phone with IBM and find out what the hell happened to the new hard drives we ordered!"

"Can you look at my thing first?" she asked, propping herself against the door frame.

"Nope," I replied, plopping into my chair and slapping the space bar on the keyboard, waking my computer from the screen saver.

She sighed heavily. "You know, you wouldn't even be here if it weren't for me!"

I scanned the monitor in front of me, catching up on the IRC conversation I'd been away from. With a purposeful motion, I looked up at her, locked on to her eyes for a moment, and said, "Thanks for the job, Darina." I then went back to looking at my monitor as if searching for a phone number.

"Look!" she snapped as she stood upright. "I can't do my job if I can't see the résumés! And I can't see the résumés because of your stupid e-mail thing! So *you're* the reason I can't do my job, which means *you* need to fix this!"

"And I will," I said, then gave a slight look of surprise at the monitor, attempting to sell a moment of "Eureka!" from finding the number I needed. I quickly grabbed the phone and tapped out a sequence of numbers that, if you spelled it out on the keypad, might have read 1-800-OUR-HAMM. Or 1-800-MT-PIANO. Or, more ostensibly, 1-800-MUSIC-NOW.

"That's how you act?" she said, putting her hands on her hips. "Just . . . pick up the phone right in the middle of our conversation?"

"Obviously," I said.

"That's just rude!" she said. "Can't you show me at least a little respect?"

"Welcome to 1-800-MUSIC-NOW," a voice said over the receiver, startling me. Usually, it was an automated voice that prompted you to press one to enter an artist's name, or two for help (or, *en español, presione tres ahora*). "My name is Jessica," she continued. "How may I help you?"

"Uh, hi, Jessica," I stammered. "I need to check on the status of an order we placed a few days ago?" I looked up at Darina and adopted a pleading expression. "*Sorry, I'm on the phone,*" I mouthed, adding a gesture toward the handset with my free hand.

Darina's mouth opened wide, and she gasped with exasperation.

"Sure, I can check on that for you," Jessica replied. "Can you give me your order number?"

"Uh . . ." I said, trying to come up with something, "I think it was O-I-C-U-8-1-2."

Jessica laughed. "Nice," she responded. "I like Halen, too, but I'm afraid I need an actual order number."

Darina stood there with her mouth gaping wide.

"Uh," I said, "I actually, um, I don't seem to have the order number here. It was for some hard drives for BOSS Systems?"

"Err . . . hard drives?" Jessica responded.

Darina continued to stand there.

"Yeah," I sort of answered. "For the IBM S/390 server."

"Well, sir, we sell music," Jessica responded. "This is 1-800-MUSIC-NOW."

"Yes, yes, that's the one!" I chuckled, acting as if I were relieved.

The other end of the phone was silent. I took that opportunity to look up at Darina, who was busy converting the ambient moisture in the air into steam with the heat of her anger. With a dismissive wave, I mouthed, "*Shut the door!*" and returned my gaze to the monitor in front of me.

I wasn't looking at Darina, but having seen her do it several times before, I imagined what she looked like as she spun ninety degrees on her heel with nearly military-style precision and marched away, leaving a trail of smoldering ozone in her wake.

"Sir?" Jessica finally said. "I'm afraid you may have dialed the wrong number . . ."

"No! Nonono!" I blurted as I stood to close the door. "Don't hang up!"

"Sir?"

The door shut softly behind me. "I am *so* sorry," I explained. "I'm at work, and I was trying to get rid of a co-worker, and I was expecting the automated-voice thingy, and when you spoke, it threw me off!" I chuckled nervously.

After a moment of silence, Jessica responded dryly, "Sir, I'm afraid abusing our service to dismiss your coworkers isn't really an approved use of our resources. I'm going to have to report you."

"Uh . . ." I said as I sat in my chair. "Report me?"

"Yes, sir."

"Report me to who?" I asked.

"Your boss," she said with a tension-breaking laugh.

I laughed in return. "You had me going there."

"How can I help you?" she asked.

"Honestly, I don't quite know that you can," I replied. "I was calling to dial in a few names of bands just to see if you guys have them. It's kind of a game I play."

She said, "Ah, stump the system, huh? I can help you with that if you want. I can look up any band you ask for and play back the clips."

"Really?" I replied. "That's pretty cool. But I'm probably going to be a while, and I don't want to eat up your whole morning."

"Oh, it's no problem," she said. "I'll have to do it with the next person who calls anyway. I might as well talk to a Halen fan while I work."

"I'm not really a Halen fan, per se," I confessed. "It's just a funny title."

"Oh . . . one of those types," she said with a chuckle.

"One of what?"

"The people who don't believe in the holiness of Halen and won't be saved when Eddie ascends into heaven."

"Oh, *God*," I said with a smile, "you're one of *those*!"

"Yep," she answered. "He's Jesus."

"God, I hope not," I said.

"Why not?"

" 'Cause if he is, then John Petrucci is Satan, and he's clearly going to win the battle and take over the earth."

"What!" she verbally sneered.

"Yeah," I continued, "and he's got big poofy hair. I won't want to be forced to wear big poofy hair when he takes over."

"You are so wrong," she answered. "Eddie plays circles around Petrucci."

"Let's put it to the test, then!" I said.

"How?"

"Dial up Van Halen's first record."

"Ohhhh . . ." she said. I could hear her smiling on the other end of the phone. She pulled it up, and the little automated man's voice went on to describe the album *Van Halen* by Van Halen. He then introduced a few tracks, one of them being "Eruption," which features every slobbering dork frat boy guitar-worshiping moron's idea of a bad-ass guitar solo.

"See!" Jessica said at the clip's conclusion. "How can you not think that's worthy of sitting beside God in heaven?"

"Because of this," I answered. "Dial up 'Change of Seasons' by Dream Theater."

The little automated man came up and introduced "Change of Seasons" by Dream Theater, then proceeded to play clips from the middle of songs that had nothing at all to do with Petrucci's solos. If we'd been arguing Mike Portnoy's drum excellence, I'd have won fair and square. But for this particular argument, it wasn't very helpful.

"Yep, totally great playing," she said sarcastically.

"That is *totally* not fair," I responded.

And so it went for the better part of an hour. Jessica and I argued about bands and music and who was better than whom. We also found some middle ground, agreeing that the first six Black Sabbath records should be dipped in gold and enshrined at Angkor Wat for worshipping throughout eternity. At the end of it, I purchased a few new releases I hadn't yet snagged.

"Okay, that's a huge order," she said, repeating back a total well in the hundreds of dollars.

"Huh," I said, somewhat oblivious to how many albums I'd agreed to buy. "Oh, well, I haven't bought any other records this month."

"Heh," she said. "It's the second."

"Yeah," I said. "I get paid on the first. Usually, I'd have spent my music budget by now."

"And what is your music budget?" she asked.

"You don't want to know," I replied.

"What are you, made of money or something?" She laughed.

"No no, I just really like music."

"But . . . you ordered No Doubt."

"Yeah?" I responded. "So what?"

"I thought you said you like *music*."

"Look, it was a gift for, uh, a friend, and shut up, okay?" I said sarcastically.

She laughed and then asked for all my order information. I gave it in a practiced cadence.

"All right, well," she said, wrapping up our call, "because you're nice, and because we both agreed on Butch Vig being a prophet and a saint, I suppose I *could* be nice and give you thirty percent off."

"Really?" I perked up. "That's pretty awesome!"

"Yeah, and I can't believe I'm going to say this, but . . ."

"What?"

"Well," she said hesitantly, "I *never* do this, but would you mind if I called you later? Like, after work?"

"Uh . . ." I said, flattered but slightly cautious. Okay, fine, I'll admit it—I wasn't cautious at all. I was all kinds of yes but didn't know how to say it without sounding retarded. "Sure, I suppose."

"You suppose?" she asked, offended.

"Well, yeah," I replied. "I mean, Halen fans calling me isn't something I normally agree to, but because you gave me thirty percent . . ."

"PSSSSSSH!" she said, and then laughed.

"All right, then," I said. "Want my number?"

"You just gave it to me," she said.

"Oh, right, with the order!" I said. "Yeah, okay . . . Talk to you later, I suppose!"

"There you go, supposing again."

"Yep. Get used to it. I suppose a lot."

She laughed. "So much that I have to get used to it? That's either a good sign or a bad one!"

I laughed in lieu of responding because I really had no response to that.

"Okay, well . . . tonight, then!" she said.

"Okay," I responded. "And thanks again for the thirty percent!"

"No problem. Thanks for calling 1-800-MUSIC-NOW, and have a great day!"

"You, too!" I said, hanging up the phone and looking for another reason to blow off work for the day.

Naturally, I was still up after three in the morning when she decided to call. But even if I don't sleep, it is a bit late to be calling someone for the first time. Or maybe it's a bit early, since it is the morning. Either way, it sits right at the bottom of the big list of "Times You Should Call People for the First Time."

"Hello?" I half said, half asked.

"Hey!" a bright voice said from the other end of the receiver.

"Who's this?"

"Uh, Jessica?" she replied.

"Who?"

"The girl from 1–800-MUSIC-NOW?"

"Oh," I replied flatly. "So this isn't Ed McMahon? Or Jesus?"

She stammered incoherently a second, then finally said, "No?"

"Those are about the only two people I can think of who I'd be happy to hear from at almost four in the morning, so . . ."

"Oh jeez, I forgot about the time zone thing . . ." she said with a small laugh. "But come on. You know you're happy I called."

"Perhaps," I replied with a chuckle of my own. Using my best nerdy scientist voice, I continued, "But I must express a certain amount of displeasure at the time that you chose to make the call."

"Well, I was out!" she playfully snapped. "I just got home and didn't want to go to bed without calling."

"Ah, need to be reminded of what good music is before you go to sleep?" I said.

"Noooo," she answered in a soft voice, "I just promised I would, and I *always* keep my word."

"That's quite honorable."

"Yeah, I guess," she said. "Mostly, I've just been thinking about you all day and didn't want to go to bed without talking to you."

My eyebrows raised, and I cocked my head to the side inquisitively. "That's a nice thing to say . . ." I offered.

"Thanks," she said, her tone noticeably more sultry. "It's true."

"Well, okay," I replied, not knowing what to say. "So what's up?"

"Nothing much, really," she answered, and began to tell me about her night. She and a few coworkers had gone out for a fun evening on the town. Which apparently was a weekly thing, because last week Deborah didn't make it, so this week she was in extra need of alcohol and "delicious boys" to take her mind off Dave, who worked up in the corporate office and had been flirting with her a lot lately but was married, so she couldn't have him, which was why Janice and Mary insisted she come out this time—and trust me, I was just as bored listening to it as you are reading it—and *then* Mark ordered shots for everyone . . .

"Well, that sounds really . . ." I said, searching for the right word to describe how stupid I felt the entire enterprise was, but without insulting her.

"What?" she said, not allowing the search to follow its course. "Not your kind of thing?"

"Not at all," I answered. "I'm much more into, like, not that."

"What do you mean?"

"I dunno," I said. "I'm not much of a drinker, for one."

"Oh," she said. Then she asked, "Wait—How old are you?"

"Twenty," I replied.

"Oh, Lord," she said. "You're just a baby!"

"I'd like to think that my diaper-wearing is strictly voluntary at this stage in life," I said with a marked decline in enthusiasm.

"Oh, well, I didn't mean it *that* way," she said. "I just meant . . ."

"What, that I'm young?" I supplied for her. "Why, how old are you?"

She hemmed and hawed. "I don't think I want to say now," she finally answered.

"What? Like, fifty or something?" I asked.

"*No!*" she said.

"Look, it's okay if you are," I replied. "I like old people. I like Werther's candies, and you guys always have some handy."

"Stop it!" she said through laughter.

"Come on, how old are you?"

She paused for a moment. "Thirty . . ."

"Oh, well, that's not old."

". . . Five," she finally added.

"Yeah, you're one foot out of the casket at thirty-five."

"You little punk!" she said with a chuckle.

We talked for a while longer, mostly about how a twenty-year-old could live on his own, and how a twenty-year-old could have a corporate job without a college degree, and how a twenty-year-old could have such "mature" perspectives on music, and, well, the whole damn conversation was about me being twenty and living the life I was living, and how "amazing" and "special" she thought all of that was.

"It sounds like you really have it together," she said.

"No, not really," I replied. "I just got lucky and get paid to do what I like doing, and it's all worked out so far."

"It's amazing," she said.

"What?"

"Just, I dunno, that someone so young could be this mature," she replied.

I laughed. "You wouldn't say that if I told you what I did to my previous employer on the day after Thanksgiving last year."

"No, really," she said. "You're like . . . perfect."

HANG. UP, I thought to myself.

"I just wish we lived closer," she added. "I think I'd like to know you."

"Oh, well," I stammered, "um . . ."

HANGUPHANGUPHANGUP! My brain went into overdrive. I immediately began seeking exits from the conversation. "That does suck and all, but hey, at least I got to order music from you," I said.

She was silent.

"So yeah, we got to chat, and that's nice, right?" I tried again.

"You don't agree with me?" she said.

"About what?"

"About knowing each other," she said.

"Well . . ." I said, verbally tugging at my collar, "I mean, we don't have to live near each other to know each other, right?"

"No," she replied, "but how do you get to really know someone if you can't see him, you know? Look him in the eye . . . see him smile . . ."

"Well, you—"

"Kiss him and hold him close?" she added.

The room started to spin. I needed out. "I don't think kissing and holding are mandatory," I quickly answered. "I mean, I hope not, anyway. I don't think I could stomach kissing and holding my friend Mike."

A few silent seconds went by, each one ticking off with a dull and hollow thud from my internal clock. Finally, she said in a markedly more chipper voice, "See, this is why I think you're great. You make me laugh."

"Thanks," I replied. "You're nice, too."

"Okay," she said, letting me off the hook, "it's really late there, I know. I'll let you get to sleep."

"Thanks," I said. "You sleep well, and thanks again for that order this morning. That made my day."

"Same here," she said. I could hear her smiling over the phone.

"All right, good night," I said. "Have a good day tomorrow."

"You, too," she said brightly, then hung up.

I'm fairly sure that, at least once in your life, you've gone a night with too little sleep followed by a need to get up too early the next morning. You're probably familiar with the dull pain in your head that doesn't so much pound as it squats over your skull and squeezes your brain like it's trying to choke you out in an MMA title bout. That feeling was a constant thing for me at that time in my life— back then I wasn't yet familiar with the nectar that is Red Bull. But the morning after that phone call was especially horrible.

The world was covered in a dull haze as I made my way around the house, trying to get myself cleaned, fed, and out the door. I walked into no fewer than four walls while on my *Family Circus*–esque trek around the house. And just after I'd put a toothbrush full of toothpaste into my mouth and worked up a nice foam, the phone rang.

I walked over to the phone as it rang a third time. Without considering the situation, I picked it up. "Hellofff?" I said through a mouth full of Aquafresh.

"Uh, hello?" Jessica said.

"Haa, uhhh. Holl ohh uh seh," I replied. I immediately spat the contents of my mouth into the trash can beside my desk. "There. Hi."

"Hi," she said glowingly.

"What's up?" I said, wiping my mouth with the floppy end of the towel wrapped around my waist.

"I just wanted to wish you a good morning," she replied.

"Oh. That's nice," I said. "Thanks!"

"You're welcome," she said. "Talk to you later!"

There was a click on the other end. I went to return the receiver to its cradle, and as I did, I noticed a large smudge of toothpaste on the receiver. I shook my head, wiped it down, and hung up the phone.

I nearly crashed into Juan in the hallway as I raced to get out of the house. "What the hell are you doing up so early?" he asked after the near-collision.

"Meeting," I replied.

"Ah. You look like shit. What time did you go to bed?"

"I dunno . . . like five? Six?"

"A meeting on an hour of sleep, huh? Good luck with that. What the hell were you doing all night?"

"*Ultima Online*," I lied. He'd never have understood if I'd told him about the crazy operator from 1-800-MUSIC-NOW calling and flirting with me all night.

"Addict," he replied with a smirk.

"Yeah, well . . . it's fun," I said.

"Heh. I hope you got enough of that online gold to help you float between jobs when they finally fire your ass." He waved me off as he entered the bathroom.

Yes, it was an annoying morning. And I should tell you that it's not that I didn't like Jessica's little good-morning call. Quite far from it—it's nice when someone calls to wish you good morning. I believe this, and I have done it myself. It's also nice when someone calls to say hi or see how your day is going, or to let you know she hopes work is going all right, or to check on how your drive home went.

Or to let you know that she checked the Weather Channel and saw there was a slight chance of storms in the afternoon and she just wanted you to be aware.

Or to let you know a certain song popped on the CD player and she thought of you.

Or to say that she smelled a cologne in the store that

reminded her of what you might wear, even though she's never once met you.

But when she does all of those things in one day—after having spoken to you twice ever—well, it's a bit creepy. And if you add up the bits of creepy over the span of, oh, a week or so, you get a full bucket o' creep. After a while, it begins to wear on your soul to the point where you simply stop answering the phone. Unless you happen to be at work, in the presence of your boss, who isn't quite privy to the cicumstance at large and disapproves of an employee ignoring calls on his work line.

"Why don't you want to talk to me?" Jessica's tear-strained voice blubbered through the receiver before I could even say hello. It had been a week solid of crap like this that had caused me to not answer the phone, and now she was wondering why I didn't want to talk to her. I had been an idiot for mentioning my employer during our first-ever phone call, but how could I have possibly known she'd be a total psycho and look up the number?

I closed my eyes as the pounding began in my brain. "Look," I said through a clenched jaw, "I'm at work right now. Can't we talk about this later?"

"Oh, we could," she snapped, "if you'd actually answer the phone!"

"I, uh . . ." I looked up at my boss. "I have my boss in my office, and we're talking about some pretty important stuff . . ."

"See!" she exclaimed, sniffling. "Making up reasons not to talk to me!"

"I don't . . ." I closed my eyes, breathed deeply, and reset myself. "It's not that I don't *want* to talk to you."

"No, really," Jessica choked out through her tears. "It's all right. I . . . I understand."

My boss, Gary, ducked his head and waved at me. "I'll come back," he said as he opened the door to my office. "When you're less . . . *busy.*"

"No, wait—Gary," I said as he exited. With a sigh, I returned my attention to the reason for my certain termination. "Look, Jessica . . ."

"It's so cute when you say my name like that," she said with a slight giggle and a severe mood swing.

"Nonono . . . oook, okay, this is serious!" I exclaimed. "This isn't supposed to be cute!"

"I know. That's what makes it so cute!"

"You, you, like . . ." I stammered with equal parts embarrassment and anger. There I stood in my first real office at my first real job, with a wacko on the other end of the line, and I couldn't even yell.

"I like what?" she asked playfully.

It was just too much. "OH MY GOD!" I snapped. "You have *got* to stop calling me! *Okay?*"

She was silent for a second. "Fine, I won't call you at work again. Okay?"

"Not just at work! Anytime! *Ever!*" I barked.

She paused. She huffed. She said, "You . . . you . . ." And then she hung up, just like that.

I stared at the wall, absorbing what I'd said. I didn't want to do that here. Not at work, and certainly not in front of my boss. I mean, I knew it had to be done, yes. And I figured that when the time presented itself, I'd be purposeful in thought and deed and, like a verbal surgeon, cut only where I needed to and keep the scarring minimal.

I slowly placed the receiver on the cradle, then gently lowered myself into my chair. I breathed a deep, cleansing breath.

My phone rang.

I let it roll to voice mail while I checked my e-mail. And then it rang again. So I began reading the day's news headlines on CNN.com.

The phone rang again. And again. And again. With each ring, a brand-new ulcer appeared in my stomach. I was already seen as having an extraneous job position at this company, and my attitude toward my detractors had done little to sway their opinion in favor of me. This was the last thing I needed.

The intercom alert sounded. "Joe?" a sweet voice asked over the speaker.

"Yeah, Yvonne?" I said to our company's receptionist with a sigh.

"I have a call for you . . . someone named Jessica?"

I growled.

"Don't want to take it, I suppose?" she said.

"Oh, sorry about that," I said, not realizing that that growl had been outside of my own brain. "Yeah, I really don't."

"No problem," she said. "I've got it covered! I'll just send her to voice mail."

"Thanks, Yvonne," I replied as my head fell into my hands.

About ten minutes went by. My phone chirped again, and Yvonne called over the speaker again.

"Yeah?" I replied, placing my middle finger and thumb on my temple in anticipation of what was coming.

"This lady, Jessica? She's uh . . . she's VERY persistent . . ."

"To say the least," I said with a grumble.

"She's really disrupting the flow of calls here. Can you please talk to her and get her to quit calling?"

"It won't work." I sighed. "But sure, put her through."

"Okay," Yvonne said as her voice gave way to a loud beep that signified the connecting of a call from the front desk, which gave way to a rather loud and, frankly, impressive string of vulgarity.

"Hey hey hey!" I said as I yanked the phone off the cradle to hang up the speaker. "Calm down!"

"CALM DOWN?" Jessica barked. "You *asshole*! I'm not going to calm down! You just tried to avoid me like a fucking coward. You can't even be a man and tell me you don't want to talk to me!"

"Uh . . . I think I *did* tell you I don't want to talk to you," I replied. "Just before you hung up on me."

"Whatever!" she shouted. "You should be man enough to face a woman when you toss her aside! You should be willing to at least explain yourself!"

I thought for a moment. "If you wanted an explanation, then why did you hang up?" I asked.

"You pissed me off!" she yelled. "You can't . . . You were totally rude!"

"Look," I said, "we cannot do this now, okay? I'm at work. You cannot keep calling me at work, all right?"

"Then stop avoiding me!" she barked.

"Right, okay, I will. Just . . . let's talk about this tonight? Please? Can you hold off calling me until then?"

She sighed. "You won't answer. You'll duck me."

"I won't, I promise." I regretted saying it the moment it came out of my mouth. I knew that promising anything to someone like her couldn't possibly be a good thing.

She thought. "Fine," she huffed. "Tonight, then." And she hung up.

For the rest of the afternoon, there was peace. But that evening was just plain awful. She called at least fifteen times before I got home. I know this because there were fifteen messages on my answering machine from a person who was slowly slipping into madness.

Just as one of the final messages was playing, the phone rang again. It was sheer force of will that made me take hold of the handset of my phone. With as cheerful a tone as I could muster, I greeted my caller. And thus sprang a cacophony of Jessica as the answering machine and the receiver of the phone simultaneously spewed the rants and raves of this crazy woman.

"Who is that in the background?" she snapped after a moment.

"It's you," I replied.

"Ha, ha, very *funny!*" she barked. "Who is it really?"

"It's you!" I said again. "It's the answering machine playing one of your eleventy-billion messages!"

"Oh," she said. "Well, turn it off. We need to talk."

"Yeah, we sure do," I answered.

And we did. For the entire conversation, I felt like a frightened Dalmatian attempting to flee the leash around its neck as it was yanked and pulled hither and yon. Why a Dalmatian? Because from a distance, they're beautiful. You think, "Wow, what a vision of beauty and majesty." So you go and you make the mistake of getting one, and it's neurotic and insane and quite possibly the worst thing you've ever let into your life. She chastised my inability to show any sort of compassion toward her during this lonely time in her life in the same breath that she screamed about my leading her on. I was an evil young man hell-bent on scoring an older woman. I'd been malevolent in my manipulation of her feelings. I was high and mighty and self-important due to the job I had and my ability to survive on my own two feet at such a young age.

And then, almost as if someone had flipped a switch, the tears began to flow. I was the best thing that had happened to her in the past few months. I was so intelligent and unique and special, and she would do anything to make up for her behavior. I was everything she never knew she wanted in a friend and "lover," and it was fate that had brought us together, and who was she to argue with fate? And who was I to rebel against it? Why couldn't I see? Why couldn't I understand? Then came the profanity.

This went on for the better part of three hours. For the entire duration, I sat as silently as possible, agreeing in the right places and allowing her to get it all out of her system. A few times she would wind down a bit, and I'd attempt to make my move to cauterize the wound and terminate the conversation (and the relationship we didn't have) only to be silenced by her renewed enthusiasm for hearing herself talk. Eventually, she ran out of steam, and I was given the chance to bring the thing down gently.

"Okay, I hear you," I said. "I do, I really do."

"Really?" she said through tears.

"Yes, really," I said. "And I want you to know, I understand where you're coming from. You're in a very difficult spot in life. You're feeling alone and unloved."

"Yes!" she said. "Exactly!"

"And you need to believe that there's someone out there for you."

"Right. I really do."

"And you need a friend. Someone who understands you."

"Exactly."

"I'm not that person, Jessica."

She was silent for a moment. "Of course you are," she said. "I mean, what you just said. That's exactly it. You get it."

"No," I replied. "I get your situation. I don't get *you*."

There was a hollowness across the line. Finally, she asked, "What do you mean?"

"You've done a great job of explaining your situation. I just repeated what you've told me. I didn't figure any of this out; you told me what was going on."

She didn't reply.

"And I don't know what to make of it," I continued. "We

don't know each other at all. We've talked a few times, and you've confided in me quite a lot. But I'll tell you, I didn't really get any of it. I mean, I heard you, but I don't know what to do with any of it. It seems like all you needed was someone to allow you to vent and get it all out. But everything I just told you? That you agreed with?"

"Yeah?" she chirped.

"You said all of that. Those were your words. You're the strong one here."

She thought for a few minutes. "I am?"

"Yeah," I said. "I'm only twenty! I don't know anything about life! I haven't been through what you've been through, in life or in love. The divorces, the abuse, the moving around, your experiences with other, you know, women . . ."

She chuckled at my naïveté, which was what I was hoping for. I had no trouble talking about lesbians—in fact, what with all the porn I'd seen up to that point, I felt like quite the expert. But playing innocent seemed to convey the point that I had no clue what life was about, as did everything I was saying. My words were all very carefully chosen and planned. And they seemed to be working.

"You have your answers," I continued. "You just needed to put a voice to them. And I'm glad I was here to help with that."

She sighed. "You're right," she said in a relieved tone. "You're so right."

And now the trump card. "I think the best thing for you, honestly, is to just take some time, right now, to be with Jessica. Be by yourself. Get to know yourself again. Disappear. Take a trip somewhere. Meditate. But get to know yourself."

"Yeah, that's a good idea," she agreed. "That's a great idea. You're so right."

"No, *you* were right," I echoed as I prayed that my plan had worked. "You're the strong one, remember?"

"Wow. Thank you. I am just . . . Wow, I'm SO embarrassed by my behavior, and you've been so wonderful to handle it and help me out."

"No problem," I said, sighing as quietly as I could so my own relief wouldn't be so evident. I placed a little bit of cheer in my voice as I said, "Now get started! Right now!"

"I will!" she said.

"Remember," I said seriously, "you need 'you time.' No one else can be as strong for you as you are. Not even me. Just Jessica and Jessica alone, right?"

"Right. You're right," she said. "Thank you."

"No problem," I said. "I'm going to go now and let you get started, all right?"

"Thanks," she said. "For everything."

"Good night, and goodbye."

"Bye," she said as she hung up.

I placed the phone on the cradle. With a heave, I flung myself on my bed and lay there, watching the ceiling fan spin nearly as fast as my head was.

The next day I was on pins and needles as I awaited the inevitable call. That night became the next morning, and the days began to accumulate to the point where you could call them a week, and there was no call. No voice mails at work; no messages on the answering machine. Nothing.

It was the eighth day of the streak and a particularly rainy Saturday. My roommates had decided to head off to do a little pawnshop-hopping for the day, and I couldn't have possibly been more pleased—it allowed me to mine for gold in *Ultima Online* without the jeers and insults. It was about eleven in the morning, and I had just settled into my game with a tall glass of iced tea when I heard a knock at the door.

It took a moment for me to realize I couldn't ignore it because the shades were open and whoever was there had already seen that I was home, so I grudgingly lifted my unmotivated frame off the floor and plodded over to the door. I opened it to find an exceptionally thin, somewhat pretty middle-aged redhead standing on the porch, a suitcase in one hand and her heart in the other.

I knew immediately who it was. "Uh, hi," I said.

She smiled and shrugged nervously. "Surprise," she said in a whisper.

"Jessica?" I asked rhetorically.

She answered anyway. "Yep. Hi."

"What, uh . . ." I began.

"Well," she said, "you said to take a trip . . . so here I am . . ."

I wanted to explode. I wanted to scream and run away. I wanted to call the police. Instead of doing all of that, I simply heard my mother's voice echoing in my head, reminding me of my proper upbringing. "Um, come in," I said, pushing the screen door open.

She did.

I didn't quite know what to say or do. "So, how did you, like, know where I lived?"

"Your order," she replied. "From MUSIC-NOW. I looked it up."

"Oh," I said in a tone that I was sure explained that I had no idea what to think of that. "And so you just, like, came out here?" My voice squeaked a little.

"Yeah," she said. "Flew in this morning."

"Well," I said, not quite sure what to say next. I began wringing my hands and shifting my weight from one foot to another as my mind spun.

"You mind if I sit down?" she asked, taking the initiative.

"Sure, go ahead," I replied. "Do you want something to drink? Or something?"

"Yeah, sure. Water would be fine." She took a seat on the couch.

I nodded, smiled nervously, and went into the kitchen to get a knife to slit my throat. But all our knives were dirty, and I was afraid of catching some sort of food-borne illness from them, so instead of slicing my jugular, I got Jessica a glass of water.

I then took a seat across from her on the beanbag chair I'd previously occupied. She drank, then smiled at me. I smiled from one side of my mouth and began staring at the floor. "This is certainly a surprise," I offered.

"Yeah," she said, putting down the glass. "I . . . I shouldn't have come."

"Possibly," I replied. "Your plan was to just show up on my doorstep and hang out for, what, the weekend?"

She shook her head. "I leave next Friday."

"A week?" I blurted out. "I mean . . . you just thought you'd show up unannounced for a week?"

She looked up at the ceiling, then back at the floor. "Something like that," she replied.

"That's—"

"Crazy," she interjected. "I know. I'm thinking the same thing right now."

"Then why?"

Her lip quivered slightly and she sighed. "I don't know," she said, picking up her water glass. "I took your advice, you know? I took some time off work, and I spent some time just, like, alone and stuff. And I knew you said you didn't want me to call, and you said to take a trip somewhere . . ." She took a sip from her glass and looked at me.

"You thought, I'll go to Atlanta, see how Joe's doing? Is that it?"

She rolled her eyes. "I know, it's stupid."

"It's not stupid," I said. "It's really, really strange."

"I dunno, Joe!" she said, setting her glass back on the floor. "I know the answers are within me, like you said. I know I have them, I just . . . I felt lost, you know? And when you talked to me that night, I felt so together. Like everything made sense."

I blinked.

She continued. "I needed that feeling again. And I felt like you may not answer the phone, you know? For my own good? Because I needed to be by myself and figure myself out? But I really needed that anchor. The grounding you provide."

I didn't say a word. Mostly because I had absolutely nothing to say.

"And I felt like, if you could just see me, know me, you know? Maybe you'd . . ." She stirred on the couch, then sighed heavily. "God, I feel so *stupid*," she exclaimed. "This is such a bad idea. I just really wasn't thinking."

"It's all right," I said. It wasn't, but saying so wouldn't have helped anything.

"I'm so sorry," she said. "I . . . Where's your phone?"

I pointed to the end table on the far side of the couch. "Why?" I asked.

"I'm going to call the airline," she said. "See if I can switch my ticket out and fly out tonight. I feel so horrible."

She reached for the phone. I watched as she dug through her bag to find her ticket and dialed the number on it. I listened as she conversed with the operator on the other end of the line. I watched as she grabbed her credit card to pay the fee for switching the flight. I sighed heavily as she hung up the phone.

"Tomorrow morning, nine-fifteen," she said. "Look—I am really, really sorry about all of this. I'm out of my mind, and I know that. But I have to ask you a favor."

"Okay," I replied flatly.

"Would you mind if . . . I mean, I just spent the rest of my money changing the ticket, and I have no place to go."

"You need a place to stay," I said.

"Yeah," she answered.

In a race for reactions, sympathy beats disgust by a nose. Before I could reconcile it within myself, I had said, "Yeah, that's fine."

"Thanks," she said with a smile. Immediately, she lay back and closed her eyes. I can't be sure, because quite frankly, my mind was in at least two hundred different places at that moment, but I'd be willing to gamble that she was asleep before her eyelids had shut. Inside of five minutes, she was snoring.

The woman was able to fall asleep in under five minutes in a complete stranger's house. A stranger whom she'd just surprised with an unannounced visit from Phoenix. As fucking loony as she was, there was a part of me that couldn't help being envious of that sort of audacity. But there was a whole other part of me that dreaded explaining all of this to the two least sympathetic people on the planet when they arrived home in a few hours.

Mike stared at his cookie, pondering the story I'd just told him. Then again, he could have been studying the pattern his teeth had made as he worked his way around a particularly large piece of walnut. I couldn't really tell. You never can with Mike.

"So . . ." I probed.

Without looking away from his cookie, he nodded.

I sighed.

"What?" he asked.

"You know what," I said as I stood up in a huff.

"What, you want to know what I think?" he asked, following my movement across the kitchen with his head.

I sighed again. "You know I do," I said as I opened the fridge to get a drink.

"Yeah, well, you already know what I think, so I don't see the point."

"Maybe I just want to talk about it?" I said from inside the fridge.

"You just spent an hour talking about it," he responded.

I grabbed a can of soda I'd been staring at for several seconds and popped its top as I kicked the refrigerator door closed behind me. "You know, for being my best friend, you really can be a dick sometimes." I turned to walk out of the kitchen.

"What, you don't want to talk now?" Mike asked.

"Nah . . . If you're not going to help me, I might as well be playing *GoldenEye* with— Oh, shit!" I whipped around to find that Mike had stood to follow me upstairs.

He stopped as fast in his tracks as I had. "What is it?" he whispered.

I signaled for him to hush and waved him down as if we were treading the jungle in search of Vietcong. Slowly, I crept into the living room, past the couch and toward the front window to confirm what I thought I'd seen. I made out what appeared to be a sneaker, which was revealed to be connected to a foot, which was fastened to a hip belonging to a crying and distraught thirty-five-year-old woman from Arizona.

"Fuck!" I whispered loudly.

Mike shrugged.

"She's on the porch," I whispered, pointing my thumb over my shoulder, indicating where both the porch and Jessica were.

"Oh, no way," Mike said aloud. Just as he did, I looked through the window to see Jessica's sneakered foot jerk slightly, acknowledging that she'd heard him.

I shot a look Mike's way. "Great."

"Sorry," he said. "But it's not like she didn't know we were home."

"I guess you're right. So, what do I do?"

"I dunno," he said. "That's a tough call."

"You know," I said, "you've been absolutely no help whatsoever today. Thank you. Really. I mean that."

"What?" he said. "You're in a fucked-up situation. Nothing I can say will help it. What do you want me to do, tell you everything is going to be all right? You've got a woman from Arizona sleeping on our doorstep. There's not much to be said, you know?"

"Yeah, I know," I replied. "I just have no idea how to handle this."

Mike looked at me. "You going to talk to her?"

"Yeah . . . I think I have to."

"You don't *have* to," he said. "You could just go upstairs and pretend she doesn't exist."

"Yeah, and then Juan gets up tomorrow and finds her sleeping on our doorstep and chases her off with a broom," I answered. "Probably not the best way to end things."

"Well, that would end it for sure," Mike replied. "But you're right, you can't just leave her out there." He patted me on the shoulder and ushered me toward the door.

Following his lead, I opened it. Jessica jerked involuntarily at the sound, then regained her sense of isolation and her entitlement to it, and with that, she forced her eyes away from me.

"Hey, uh, you okay?" I said.

"What do you care?" she said through her sniffles.

I didn't really have an answer for that question, so I asked one of my own. "What are you going to do?"

"What *can* I do?" she cried. "I don't have any money for a hotel room, and even if I did, I have no idea where a pay phone is, so I can't call a cab. You and your roommates are total dickheads, so I can't use your phone . . ."

"Oh, come on," I barely got to say.

"No!" she screamed. She continued saying "no" as she fumbled around and stood up, discovering slightly too late that her left leg had fallen asleep—but that didn't deter her. "You are such a *prick,*" she said, throwing her finger into my chest. "You pretend to be all supportive and helpful! You pretend you have my best interests at heart! And then you call me fucking *crazy* to your asshole friends!"

"Look, that was taken out of context."

"How can 'crazy' be taken out of context?" she barked.

I immediately began constructing an argument based on how I'd said that coming here with no notice or permission was a crazy idea, not that *she* was crazy, but I couldn't bring myself to lie. So I danced around the subject and brought up as many other subjects as I could to try to lighten the impact of having called her crazy, which had the same result as switching from a baseball bat to a pillow when whacking a hornet's nest.

We argued for a good ten minutes. Then she cried for three. Then we argued for another seven. Then some crying, and then some apologizing, and then some acquiescence, and then the inevitable: "So can I stay here?"

I sighed. I turned around. I opened the door.

Mike was standing there. "You know, Juan's going to freak if you invite her in," he said, reading it on my face before I could even tell him what was up.

"You're right, but what am I supposed to do? Just leave her out there?"

Mike looked at me as plainly as he'd ever looked at me at any point in my life. "Yes," he said.

"Hey, fuck you!" Jessica said from behind me.

"Hey now!" I said, whipping around to face her. "Chill out!"

"He's being a dick!" she said.

"Whatever, ignore him," I said. I turned back to Mike. I narrowed my eyes at him. "Would *you*?"

He studied me like a cookie. "Probably not," he finally answered.

I walked Jessica up to my bedroom. "You can sleep here," I said, showing her the bed.

"Uh, no, she can't," I heard from the end of the hall. Mike had gone to break the news to Juan, who had come to break some news of his own.

"Dude, she has no place else to go," I said.

"How about the Salvation Army?" he said.

"Come on."

"No," he snapped. "Seriously, dude? Crazy McBatshit can't stay here."

"What did you just call me?" Jessica screamed.

"Okay, stop! Both of you!" I demanded. "Juan—she's sleeping in my room tonight. You can lock your door if you want."

"But what about—" he said, clearly about to mention

the downstairs television and Nintendo and other things that could be stolen.

"She can't take a TV on the plane," I replied. "Just chill, okay? Jessica?" I turned to face her. "You're going to sleep in there, and come eight tomorrow morning, you're taking a cab to the airport. All right?"

"Fine," she said, marching into the room and slamming the door behind her.

Juan looked at me in disbelief for allowing a stalker to sleep in our house. Mike looked at me in disbelief for snapping at Juan. I looked at the floor in disbelief that this was even happening.

"You know, I'm not going to come to your funeral after she stabs you in your sleep tonight," Juan said as he returned to his room and, like Jessica, slammed the door behind him.

I walked into my office and pulled out the futon, then grabbed a notebook and began scribbling furiously in it. I was angry that I had to start a new notebook, as my current journal was sitting on the shelf in my bedroom along with the rest of my old journals and notebooks and sketchbooks. But I wasn't about to go knock on the door and ask for it.

I won't lie—the entire night, I fully expected to hear a knock on my office door. I believed with all my heart that Jessica was going to interrupt my post-midnight writing session to tell me how sorry she was, or how she couldn't sleep, or how she hated my guts. I knew that at any moment, she'd lightly tap on the door and ask to sneak in so we could talk things out, and I'd tell her how there was nothing to talk about, and she'd reply that there was and slowly let the sleeve on her oversize shirt slip down her left shoulder . . .

But I'd be strong. It didn't matter how much this chick wanted me, I didn't need a crazy older woman banging on my door and then banging me. No, sir. Not even slightly. Okay, well, slightly. But not enough to go through with it . . . Definitely not enough to get caught doing it by Juan or Mike. So if we DID do it—which I probably wouldn't—we'd have to be very quiet. It'd have to be slow and silent and—

KNOCK KNOCK.

My head shot up from my notebook. I walked over to the door. Quietly, I opened it to find Jessica standing there. "Joe . . ." she whispered.

"Go back to bed, Jessica," I replied.

"But I—"

"Go," I said, shutting the door.

I didn't sleep a wink that night for fear that she might knock again, or jump out a window, or set the house on fire. Eight o'clock came, and with it, the slamming of my bedroom door. I heard some clunking and thumping on the stairs, followed by the opening and slamming of the front door. I sat up on my futon and walked over to the window to see a taxi sitting in the driveway and a thirty-five-year-old woman climbing into the backseat. She looked up at the window I was staring out of, raised her right hand, and extended her middle finger. And as with every other door she'd come in contact with in the past twelve hours, she slammed the door of the cab as it backed out of our driveway and took Jessica out of my life forever.

With a heavy sigh, I flopped onto my futon and slept more restfully than I had in a good, long while.

It wasn't until a few months later that I noticed they were gone.

I looked at the gap in the piles of notebooks on my bedroom shelf for several minutes, trying to mentally place where I may have moved the missing journals. Sometimes I'd take out a stack and reread them, tracing through the moments of my life that I'd felt were noteworthy—could I have left them in the office? No, probably not. Maybe Mike or Juan had taken them? No, they were good guys; they stayed out of my business.

And then it hit me: Jessica. I hadn't thought about her in a while, but the second I did, my guts churned and I wanted to vomit. She'd slept in my room exactly one night and had with her a suitcase and plenty of motivation to take some sort of souvenir of her insane trip to Atlanta.

I really really wanted those journals back. But to be honest, it was worth losing nearly three years of my life's scribblings to never, ever hear from her again. There was no telling what it would have sparked—who knows, maybe she took them so I'd call her. If so, she'd get no such satisfaction from me. And if she stole them to read through my life, well, by waiting a few years, she could have fired up her Web browser and done it without the expense of a plane ticket to Atlanta.

Naturally, you could have knocked me over with a can of compressed air when the journals mysteriously showed up one cold January morning in 2008. I have my P.O. box on my Web site, and it's no strange occurrence to get a package or postcard from a reader or a friend. Rather routinely, I'd begun opening the packages I'd received that morning, and boom—a stack of my own journals. Even though there was no return address, there was only one place they could have come from.

Of course, my wife asked what was in the box, so I had to tell her. I also had to tell her where they'd come from, and how they'd come to be in Jessica's possession, and how I'd met her. My wife had heard bits of the story before, but never the whole thing in one sitting. It took the entire afternoon.

"So Jessica stole these?" Andrea asked as she shuffled through the box of journals sitting on our dining room table.

"Looks that way," I replied.

"Wow." My wife sat there, stunned.

"Yeah," I said. "Kinda fucked up, huh?"

"Just . . . wow."

"I know, right?" I said, pulling the last three of the notebooks out of the Styrofoam-peanut-filled box. There was no letter. There was no rhyme or reason for them to suddenly appear. "I just wonder why now?"

"What do you mean?" Andrea asked.

"It's been over ten years, you know? No calls, no letters, no nothing. She left me alone all this time. Why send these to me now? Why not, like, the next month or the next year or 2002 or something?"

"I dunno," Andrea said.

We both sat there, considering the situation. I wanted to get up and get on with my day, but I couldn't. This was so inexplicable and unexpected. It had taken me by surprise and forced me to revisit a story I'd worked so hard to forget.

Finally, my wife spoke. "Maybe she looked you up and found your site? And maybe she feels like the stuff in those notebooks isn't as special now that it's out on the Net?"

"Huh?" I asked after a lengthy pause.

"Well, look at it," she said. "This is all stuff from when you were in high school, and you've written about a lot of it. Now everyone knows about the pukey blow job and Wal-Mart and that girl Amanda and the student teacher . . ."

"Huh," I said.

"I don't know," she added, "but I do know that if she ever does show up again, I'm going to give up my stance against guns and learn to use the twelve-gauge."

I smirked. I couldn't help but love seeing her defensive of me. With a certain sense of bewilderment and satisfaction, I marched the box of journals upstairs and reshuffled my storage bookshelf to make room for them with the other notebooks, right where they belong.

CHAPTER 5

WHERE'S YOUR SENSE OF ADVENTURE?

"Free," I said with a smile.

The thoroughly pierced hippie woman looked at me queerly (and I'm not using that term because she was wearing a green shirt with white lettering proclaiming WHY, YES, I'M A DYKE!, I promise).

"Um . . . pardon?" she said in reply to my reply.

I smiled slightly. "You asked me how I am, and, uh . . ."

"What?" she asked.

"Never mind," I settled on as my answer. I knew that any attempt to explain to her what it had taken for me to arrive at that café would be met with more askance looks.

She tapped her pen on the side of her notepad. "All right, then. What'll you have?"

"Um, what's good?" I asked, picking up a menu.

"I dunno," she said. "A lot of people like the couscous."

"Is the couscous good?"

"I don't like it."

"So it's not good?" I asked.

"Well, a lot of people like it," she responded, tapping her pen against her pad again.

I pondered the situation. Here I was, being sold a plate of couscous whose only selling point was the fact that everyone except the waitress liked it. I didn't even know what the hell couscous was. I mean, I'd never been in an Indian restaurant before that moment. But I was feeling adventurous. Exploratory.

Free.

"What the hell, I'll try it," I said with a slight smile.

"You got it," she said as she turned to go put in my order.

The whole interaction was different from any I'd have in a restaurant at home. It was off-kilter and unbalancing. But different, I decided, was good. Given the fact that my decision to take this gig out in San Francisco had been based on shaking things up and changing the status quo of my life, it was exactly what I needed. Besides, it beat the holy shit out of the tiny room I'd practically barricaded myself in since I'd arrived.

It was horrific. Sitting there in that room, I knew that a glorious and exciting new city lay just beyond the door of my apartment. And I wanted to experience it. Oh, more than anything, I wanted to soak myself in the culture and the vibrance and the excitement of San Francisco. I'd even done some research before I flew out to find an area of town that best fit with my interests, settling on Haight Street, just a half mile south of the famous Haight-Ashbury neighborhood. My place was a tiny little walk-up near Divisadero Street, an "apartment" I subleased from a lady I knew from the chat room I frequented at the time. It wasn't cheap, but hey, my employer was footing the bill, and I had no trouble whatsoever with spending BOSS Systems's money.

I did, however, have trouble leaving the apartment. I wasn't used to traveling alone. I mean, I'd taken a drive up to Chattanooga by myself before, but other than that, this was my first trip out of Georgia. However, now I had a corporate American Express card. And before I'd come out here, Gary had told me that if I kept the monthly expenses below five digits, he'd sign off on anything I purchased.

Still, for the past two days, each time I brought myself to the point where I was ready to go out and explore the city, I found something else to stall my departure. I'd showered, but I couldn't go out until my hair was fully dry. And once it was, I'd happen to find an interesting show on television . . . And once that was over, well, it was time to eat, but I had no idea what was around my new apartment, so maybe I should order a pizza . . . And once that came, I was too full to walk around, so I decided to just go out the next day . . . And as Thursday became Friday, and Friday became the weekend, I started to realize I was pathetic.

I didn't need my friends to go with me for support, or anyone's permission to go out and have fun. I was a grown-up, and by George, all I needed was to man up and get out of that apartment on my own and do some new, exciting stuff in a new, exciting city. So Saturday afternoon, I put on a jacket and walked out the front door. I had no idea where I was going or what I was going to do besides get the hell out of my apartment and—at the very least—get something to eat.

Fortunately for me, there was a little Indian café up across the street from my temporary home. And that was where I first tried couscous, a dish that isn't even Indian. But it was there, and it was new, and I was being adventurous.

"You know, this is really good," I told the young pierced-up waitress as she came to refill my glass of water.

"Nasty," she said, sticking out her tongue in seemingly involuntary disgust.

"Okay, fair enough," I replied, not knowing what more to say. "You mind if I ask you a question?"

"What do you want to know?"

"What is there to do around here?" I asked.

"This is the Haight . . . There's a lot to do here."

"Like what?"

"Well, what do you like to do?" she asked.

"I dunno. I'm looking for something cool and unusual."

"You've come to the right place," she said.

"Yeah?"

"Just turn left when you walk out of here and start walking. It'll find you."

I was confused. "What will?"

"I dunno," she said strangely. "Whatever you're looking for. It's all here." With that, she plopped my check down on the table and walked away.

As qu—um, strange as she might have been, the waitress's advice was right on. As soon as I left the café, I began to encounter cool sight after cool sight. I saw a sign for a comic book store on Divisadero that had some of the back issues of *Cerebus* I'd been hunting for months, and a really great (but very tiny) record shop that had a ton of old Mr. Bungle LPs—originals, in fact. When I asked the clerk about the collection of old Black Flag LPs I had on my want list, he said, "They probably have them down at Amoeba."

"Amoeba?"

"Yeah, man, Amoeba Music!" he said, looking and sounding very much like a hippie from central casting. "It's an old bowling alley that's been turned into a gigantic record store, man—it's far out!"

"I'll check it out. How do I get there?"

"Just take a left out of here, man, and keep walking—you'll find it!"

So I did. And on my way to Amoeba Music, I ran into a gift shop that carried tons of stickers and buttons for old punk and rock acts, as well as novel gifts that would be perfect to bring back to my friends. After that, I found a neat gelato shop selling the tastiest tiramisu-flavored scoops I'd ever had, before or since.

When I did get to Amoeba Music, I was greeted by the single largest collection of music for sale I'd ever seen in my life. It's no exaggeration to say that this place was the size of two Costco warehouses, stocked only with records, cassettes, and CDs. A few hundred dollars later, I was the proud owner of just about every rare LP and CD made in the nineties that I could have named at the time. To say I was satisfied with how the day was going would be true, but there was something more than happiness at play. I would almost say that I was proud of myself. I'd gotten over myself and ventured out on my own and explored this brand-new territory.

What better way to commemorate that event than with a tattoo, right?

Yeah, I know now that it wasn't the greatest idea. Tattoos are things you get after months and years of thinking over what it is you want inked into your skin for the rest of your life, not tokens of whims to commemorate the day you stopped being a coward and went walking around a city. But having gotten my first tattoo a few months before my trip to San Francisco, I was begging for an excuse to get another, and this seemed like exactly the right reason. Lucky for me, there was a tattoo parlor just across the street.

I walked into the clean and extremely well lit store with eight bags of merchandise in tow, and I was greeted with the looks one should expect from a bunch of grizzled tattoo and piercing artists when one is twenty-one years old, carrying eight bags of merchandise, bright-eyed and eager to get a permanent reminder of an afternoon's worth of adventure. Dismissive, jaded, annoyed—take your pick.

"Can I help you?" asked a wafer-thin Bettie Page look-alike. She had more piercings than Bettie had, and more tattoos than Bettie had, and less cleavage than Bettie had. But the haircut—that was right on.

"I'm looking to get a tattoo," I said.

Without missing a beat, she reached behind the counter and produced a clipboard with a stack of documents on it. "Sign these," she said sharply.

I began filling out the forms. There were release forms, proof-of-age forms, forms that explained the health code— tons and tons of forms. Looking back on them now, I'm not so sure that I didn't end up adopting a dog during the whole thing. A good fifteen minutes later, I slid the clipboard filled with completed forms back toward her. She asked for my driver's license and went to make a photocopy of it. "Look through those books, see if anything interests you," she said without even looking my way.

I began looking at the photo albums for the various artists in the shop. After about ten minutes of flipping through what was available, I decided that Marcus was the best of the bunch. His work had an original feel to it, as if it had been done with more artistic vision than jaded monotony. I saw works in his photo album that weren't just repeats of E-11 and C-24 from the flash art on the walls. Perhaps, I thought, I'd found the man who could do the piece I'd always wanted.

"Over here." The Bettie Page wannabe waved at me from my right.

I walked over toward her and was quickly asked what I was looking at getting done. "I'm not sure, but I think I want to talk to Marcus about a piece," I replied.

"You're looking for me?" a short, curly-haired man said from just beside Bettie Page, Jr.

"You're Marcus?" I asked.

"Yup!" he said jovially, reaching out for a handshake. "What can I do for you?"

"Well," I said, "I'm thinking about getting some work done."

"Cool, cool," he said with a practiced nod and a few years of customer service under his belt. "You got some artwork with you?"

I considered talking to him about the Akira-themed

piece I had been sketching for the past few years, but it wasn't quite where I wanted it. Besides, I wasn't entirely sold on getting an anime-themed piece. I mean, people might laugh at me (of course, ten years later, I went ahead and did it, then posted pictures all over the Internet and ended up in *Wired* magazine. And people laughed anyway).

"No artwork with me," I replied. "But I was looking at your work, and there's a theme I've wanted to work on. I was hoping maybe we could collaborate?"

"Whatcha got in mind?" he asked, leading me back to the rear of the store where his drawing desk sat.

"Well . . ." It was then that I began describing a story I'd been working on for a comic I'd planned to draw during my downtime in San Francisco. The plot of the comic was rather elaborate (overly so, when I think back on it with an adult mind) but had quite a lot to do with gateways and portals to faraway places and distant lands. I described one of the gates I had in mind, and he instantly seized on it.

"Man, that could make a pretty righteous back piece," he said. "You could do the top of the gate up around the shoulder blades and have it go down the back all the way to the waist." He sat down at his drawing desk and began sketching something.

"That'd be . . . uh . . . that's pretty big," I said with a marked note of anxiety.

He paused and looked up at me. "It doesn't have to be," he said. "It's your piece. If you want it on the shoulder or on the forearm . . ."

I looked down at what he had sketched. As soon as I saw it, the power and energy of the day's adventurousness hit me full force. A full-back tattoo: It was crazy. "Let's do the full back!" I said excitedly.

"You sure?" he said, smiling and reflecting my newfound excitement. "Great, man!" He patted me on the shoulder. "That's what I was hoping you'd say!" With that, the two of us began designing what would be the largest individual symbol of my newfound sense of daring.

A few hours later, we stood back from the drawing desk, stretching our backs, which had become stiff and cramped from such a long period of time arched over our work. We shook out our arms and our shoulders; we blinked a bit. With refreshed eyes, we returned to give the work a fresh look.

It was beautiful.

At the time it was definitely one of the wickedest, most profound things I'd seen committed to paper—and it was made even more so from the dueling pencils that Marcus and I had wielded in concert. It was a fantastic representation of the story line I had been working on. My detail work in the patterns of the wrought-iron fencing for the gateway had been brought to life by his subtle shading, and his background work was unbelievable. The entrance into the next plane of existence had never looked so clear. I'd never thought to place the statues of heroes past and other symbols beyond the gate, but he assured me it would make for a more interesting piece.

"And you're sure it'll look like this when it's on my back?" I asked him.

"Oh, no doubt, man," he replied, removing his cap and brushing through his thick brown locks with his fingers. "Just understand, this is definitely a multiple-day job."

"Oh, yeah, definitely," I agreed. "I wouldn't expect you to be able to do all this in . . . uh . . . what time do you close?"

"Nine," he answered.

"Yeah, so, like, three hours? No way."

He chuckled. "We'll be doing good to get it done in three days, man."

My eyes opened wide. "Three solid days?" I asked, remembering how uncomfortable it had felt to sit three hours for the tiny Japanese symbol on my left shoulder.

"Oh, no way," he replied. "It'll take at least two weeks between sessions to let the area heal up and let the new skin peel. You're talking about six weeks or so."

"Oh, wow. Well, I'm here for the next few months, so I guess that won't be a problem."

"Cool," he said, replacing his cap on his head. "So, when do you want to start?"

I gave him a sideways look. "How about right now?" I said.

He laughed. "Dude, come on! Today's my birthday! You're lucky you even caught me in here today. I'm supposed to be off."

"That really sucks—I'm sorry, man!"

"Yeah, and I only agreed to come in for a quick morning sitting, but then you showed up and ruined my afternoon."

"Dude," I replied passively, "why didn't you say something? I could have come back."

He patted me on the shoulder. "I'm kidding, man. It was great. It's nice to get to do some original work."

"At least it was fun," I replied.

"Heh," he said. "I'm just glad I was wrong about you."

"What do you mean?"

"The second I saw you, I had you pegged as one of those jocks who wanted a damn Chinese character or something."

I ducked my head and grinned.

"What?" he asked.

I slowly lifted my left shirtsleeve in reply.

"Oh, man," he said, shocked but laughing. "I am so sorry! I didn't mean to insult you."

"Hey, don't be," I said. "I was eighteen."

"Say no more!" he said, slapping me on the arm again. "You know what? Fuck it. My party doesn't start until ten anyway. Let's fucking bang out some of the outline."

"Really?" I asked, delighted.

"Hell, yeah, man," he answered. "I'm stoked to do this thing here. We can get the outline going and some of the detail work in that masthead if you want."

"Hell, yeah," I echoed. "But if it's okay, I'd like to start with stuff that can be, you know . . ."

"Oh," he said, reading my mind. "You'll be able to walk around with it. I won't just leave you with a bunch of black lines."

"Rad," I answered.

We went back to the tattooing studio, and he had me sit on a piece of furniture that very much resembled a dentist's chair, only wider. I waited as he set up his tray and needles, and I watched as he got his instrumentation dialed in and his inks set up. About forty minutes later, we were ready to work.

There's something odd that happens when you're being jabbed in the spine multiple times with a gigantic needle. The constant reminder that you're in pain slows the passage of time to a crawl. It felt like I'd been lying there for a century or maybe even two. In reality, it had been nearly two hours. At last he sat back, sighed, and told me that we were done for the night.

"Yeah?" I asked, half inquisitive and half relieved.

"Yeah," he replied. "Stand up and take a look."

I stood as he handed me a large mirror. I looked at the reflection of my reflection in the large wall mirror behind me, and what I saw left me underwhelmed. "Wow," I said, reacting to the black lines that framed the top part of the door on the gateway.

He could hear the disappointment in my voice. "I know," he said. "Doesn't look like much, but really, it's a lot of the important stuff."

"I dunno," I said. "The circle decoration from the top center part looks neat, and I'm glad that's done and filled in. But the line work . . ."

"Yeah, I know," he repeated.

"It just felt like a lot more was done, you know?"

He nodded. "I do indeed. But hey, some good ground-work was laid tonight."

I shrugged. "Eh, well, here's to a really good start, right?" I said, trying to sound cheerful.

"Right," he said, smiling. "It's cool, man, we're going to get a lot more knocked out tomorrow."

"Cool," I replied as he began rubbing the new ink and

line work with some A+D ointment. "I'm really looking forward to this. I can already see it in my mind."

We shook hands and I wished him well at his party, then I put on my shirt and left to pay the Bettie Page chick at the front of the store. I left the store and headed home with all of the trophies and markings won from a day full of adventure.

I awoke the next morning sore but eager to face the new day. The rush one gets from overcoming his own trappings and shortcomings isn't easily lost—it lasts for as long as one can keep recapturing that moment. In a city like San Francisco, with a new outlook on my new neighborhood and a back full of new art to receive, I was primed to carry the feeling through the next few months.

I got dressed and strode out of the apartment with an air of confidence. I smiled as I trotted down Haight Street toward the tattoo parlor. I wasn't exactly looking forward to the feeling of my spine being treated like a hunk of city street by a jackhammer. But the end result would be worth it. There would be something uniquely mine on my back for me to carry wherever I went. A permanent piece of equipment, the framework of my courage.

I practically crashed through the front door of the tattoo parlor. From the inside, I probably looked as though I thought I was Fonzie from *Happy Days* entering Al's diner. The Bettie Page girl from the night before was standing behind the counter. I approached with a swagger and tapped out a quick rhythm on the counter in front of her. "Heya," I said, chipper as could be.

She didn't reply.

I shifted my weight between each of my feet for a second or two. "So, where's Marcus?" I asked in a light-hearted tone. "I'm ready to get this show on the road."

She immediately placed her face in her palms and began sobbing. I heard her mumble something. It sounded like someone chewing on an overcooked mouse.

"Excuse me?" I said politely.

Her head shot up, and she looked at me as if I'd just thrown a dart into her best friend's ass. There were black streams winding their way down her blushed cheekbones. Her neck was a fiery red, and a pasty mixture of white makeup and teardrops pooled at her jawline. "I said he's dead!" she barked.

"What?" I asked. Not so much because I didn't understand her but because my brain had performed an immediate lockdown—absolutely no new information was allowed in or out of it.

"Can you not *hear*?" she practically screamed. "Do I have to write it out for you?"

"Sir," I heard from behind me. I turned to find a tall, lanky man in a draping beach shirt, some cargo pants, and a pair of sandals. "Are you here for an appointment?"

"Yeah," I replied. "I was supposed to . . . Wait, so, like, Marcus died?"

"*God!*" the Bettie Page girl yelped from behind me. She then became overwhelmed and burst into tears again.

"You'd better come with me," the man said, touching my arm lightly.

I staggered behind him, bewildered by what was happening. As I looked around, I noted the sullen faces of all of the employees. They were all very clearly shaken up—the piercing lady was hugging one of the counter workers; two tattoo artists sat in chairs across from each other with their elbows on their knees and their heads hung between their shoulders. Another person sat in the corner, staring out the window of the parlor.

"Have a seat," he said as we dipped behind the curtain of the studio. I sat in the same chair I'd been tattooed in the night before. "This is so hard . . ." He began to choke up.

"I imagine," I replied, hoping to sound somewhat sympathetic.

"We just . . . I mean . . . Okay, basically, Marcus was hit by a bus last night."

"Oh, my God!" I said. "Is he okay?" I felt like such a cock. I knew the answer before I'd even asked the question—it was just a reaction, completely involuntary. But it had come out, and now I had this man who was being so kind staring at me as if I'd just fallen out of the back end of a stray dog.

"He died last night," the man answered.

"I . . . I know," I blurted out. "I mean, like . . . It was just . . . I'm sorry."

He held his hand up, waving off my explanation. "It's okay, I understand," he said politely.

"Man, I am so sorry," I said.

"It's going to be hard here without him," the man said.

"Wait, why are you still open?" I asked. "You should all be at home. This is a pretty intense thing."

"We can't close," the man answered. "We're a franchise. There're rules."

I took a deep breath as the two of us sat in silence for several moments. I debated letting it go, but my curiosity got the better of me. "How did it happen?" I asked, adding, "If you don't mind?"

He took a deep breath. "We were all out for his birthday. We all had a lot to drink. It happened so fast . . . He was such a great guy!" He broke down in tears momentarily before regaining his composure. "He was my best artist."

I nodded. "He was very talented. We worked on a piece last night together."

"I saw that," he said. "It looked very impressive. It would have been a great piece."

I shifted in my seat. A nagging question had entered my mind the moment I realized Marcus had been loosed from this mortal coil, one that I didn't even want to admit to myself that I was asking. But it was there. I could feel it creeping from the depths of my subconscious, slowly working its way from the inner core of my mind, down the brain stem and into my throat.

"Speaking of that," I felt myself say.

He looked up at me, knowing full well what I was about to ask and wearing his reaction to my unspoken question clearly on his face.

I shifted in my seat again. "Like, well, the piece is unfinished . . ."

"You want a refund," he said with disappointment—not just in me but in the selfishness inherent in the entire human race.

"No!" I exclaimed. "That's not what I was going to ask."

God, I was such a liar.

•

He looked up at me. "What, then?"

"Well, I mean . . ." I coughed slightly. "Is there, like . . . Can someone in here finish this?"

He thought for a moment. "Let me see?" he asked.

I took off my shirt and showed him where we'd left off.

"I hate to say this, but honestly, looking at the artwork, I really doubt it," the man said.

I felt a dread creep up within me.

"But I'm sure we could do *something*," he said.

We went on to discuss the possibilities. He mentioned that someone in the shop might be able to connect up the lines and basically cover them with a design that would cap off the existing circle motif. He assured me that it wouldn't look like a shoddy cover job and that I wouldn't have to feel ashamed to have an unfinished tattoo on my back.

I wasn't thinking much about the future. I wasn't thinking about the fact that I could probably find a high-quality artist to pick up where this one had left off. I wasn't thinking about the fact that if I could just be patient, I would be able to take the motif and finish it.

No. Panic and dread over the idea of having a blob of black lines and a circular motif with no shading led me to agree to allow one of his artists to cover up the beginnings of the masterwork. On the house, no less.

The end product wasn't horrible, I said to myself after four hours of having a hairy-armed beast of a man bear down on my back with another huge needle. It looked like a semi-Gaelic Asian-fusion tribal sort of thing. Not ugly. Not particularly notable. Just a black conglomeration of lines on my shoulders with a circular motif in the center.

I'm certain that only I look at it and can see where it was once the beginnings of the top of a beautiful gateway to a far-off land. To everyone else, it's something to be polite about. But even after all the tattoo work I've had done since, I haven't brought myself to have it covered. It is, after all, a souvenir from one of the greatest trips I'd ever taken—a trip through the doorway from fear to adventure.

⟡

CHAPTER 6

I NEVER REALLY WAS THE OUTDOORS TYPE

We were seniors in high school, but our parents should have known better than to let Mike and me go camping on our own. Camping involves knowing how to survive, which involves knowing how to build a fire—and given that we'd burned down a Hooters restaurant the summer before, it didn't make sense that my parents would be okay with it.

But they were. And in order to go camping, I needed supplies. Both Mike and my father were outdoorsy types; Mike was an Eagle Scout, and my father loved hunting and killing and the smell of pine and whatever. But me? The closest I'd ever come to being outdoorsy was playing that horrid *E.T.* Atari game and getting him lost in the woods, and the only hunting I'd ever done was on *Duck Hunt*.

The weekend before we were to head off into the woods and live off the land, Mike and Dad and I hopped into my parents' Volkswagen Vanagon and headed up to the scout hut to pick up some gear for me to use on this trip. During the drive up, I could feel myself getting weaker from withdrawal from my Super Nintendo. When we arrived, Mike and Dad bounded out of the van with the giddiness only outdoors lovers could have for objects made of canvas and steel and smelled of DEET.

The scout hut was a camper's heaven. A cache of tents, cots, cooking stoves, lamps, fold-up chairs: All the things any outdoorsy person could ever want or need were located in this scout hut. I couldn't possibly have cared any less. I just knew I didn't want to be lying on dirt and sticks when my girlfriend, Michele, met up with me and I ditched Mike and made the trip worth going on as we sneaked off to, like, not camp. So I just agreed to whatever Mike and Dad suggested I needed and helped carry it all back to the van.

On the ride back home, I was rifling through one of the backpacks they'd picked up. In one of the pockets was a package of matches and a can with the word "Sterno" written on the side.

"What's a Sterno?" I asked Mike and Dad.

"It's not 'a' Sterno, it's just 'Sterno,'" my father noted from the front seat.

"It's fuel for the stove," Mike said.

"What, so it's, like, flammable?" I asked.

My father snorted. "It wouldn't be much good in a stove if it weren't, now, would it?"

Mike laughed and shook his head. I suppose it must have felt good for him, being knowledgeable about something I wasn't. It was a rare case—since we'd met, we'd always been the same level of smart on the same stuff. It must have felt great for his ego to get one up on me with this whole camping gambit, that fucker.

It was with all due haste that I opened the lid on the can of Sterno and dumped almost half of the contents in Mike's lap. He immediately freaked and slapped the can from my hand, causing it to spill all over the floor.

"What the *fuck*?" he yelped.

I grabbed the matchbox from the backpack, picked a match from the box, and placed it against the striking strip. "Laugh at me, will you?" I said with a manic smile.

"Oh, shit, no!" he shouted.

"Makes you feel like a big guy, knowing what Sterno is, huh?"

"Dude, don't do it!" he begged.

I wasn't going to. I just wanted him to think I would. And I carried out that illusion to the best of my ability. "You laughed at the wrong city boy, tough guy!" I said with a smirk.

"I didn't mean it," he said, attempting to wipe the Sterno off his corduroys. "Don't do it."

"What the hell?" my dad shouted from the front seat. "What is that smell? Is that the— Did you open that Sterno?"

"Yeah," I replied.

"He dumped it all over my pants!" Mike barked.

"What?" my dad said, turning back to look. He saw me holding the match to the box and Mike frantically trying to wipe his pants off with his bare hands. "What the HELL are you doing?"

"Teaching this dickhead a lesson!" I said. I thought maybe my father would understand the situation and realize that I was goofing around, given that my entire life had been spent goofing around. But when I look back on it now, I realize that my entire life had been spent attempting to goof around while actually causing reckless mayhem and strife. Usually involving fire and always by accident. Which is why I don't blame my dad for immediately reaching back to snatch the match from my hand.

But in doing so, he pulled his entire body across the steering wheel, which he held with one hand. This caused the Vanagon to swerve into the lane next to ours, which caused the driver of the car he almost creamed to lay on his horn and, presumably, scream vulgarities out the window of his vehicle. This of course caused my dad to compensate and swing the van's steering wheel the opposite direction, which pulled the vehicle left and back into our lane, but caused those of us inside to lurch hard to the right.

This knocked Mike into my left arm, which held the box of matches, which caused the box to rake across the head of the match I held in my right hand. Simultaneously, I lost my grip on both the matchbox and the matches, and they fell right into Mike's lap.

Immediately, my best friend's pants caught on fire.

"Wha . . . Augh! OH, FUCK! I'm on fire!" Mike said as calmly as he could.

"What the HELL!" my father yelled. "Did you . . . Is he on *fire*?"

I didn't reply, as I was frantically trying to slap my best friend's crotch to put out the flames.

"Ow! Shit . . . Don't . . . You're racking me!" Mike yelled.

"Sorry!" I said, continuing to slap him on the lap.

Mike dropped to the floor in front of the bench seat. Lying facedown, he began rolling on the floor of the Vanagon. Given the shitty quality of the nearly plastic fabric on the floorboard of your late-seventies model orange Volkswagen Vanagon, and given that said shitty fabric was coated in the Sterno that Mike had just knocked from my hands, it wasn't a pretty sight.

My father had just pulled the van to the side of the road when Mike performed his "stop, drop, and roll into even more fire" routine, so I leaped up and opened the van door. I dragged Mike out and plopped him on the ground, where he began unbuckling his pants. My dad joined us just as we put out the fire in Mike's pants, and he was pretty damn angry. But then he realized there was a bigger, much worse fire burning in the Volkswagen, and all he could do was watch. There was no way to put out the flames besides grabbing me and using my body to smother the fire—which, I swear to God, he was considering as he stared me down.

Poor Mike stood there in his underwear with a slightly blistered crotch. The police and firefighters arrived in time to keep the entire van from being a total loss. The seats were melted, and the upholstery was almost entirely turned into carbon (and soaking wet). But the van still ran, and after a few visits to a few junkyards, the van was suitable for travel once again (even though it stank like hell).

My parents forbade us go camping for as long as I lived under their roof, so the great "Weekend of My Birthday During Our Senior Year" camping trip was off. But considering that my first attempt at being an outdoorsman had resulted in my shooting the truck in the engine, and my second had just reduced our van to a charred hulk, nearly everyone associated with me—including myself—gave up on the idea of my ever being the outdoors type.

CHAPTER 7

SORRY, DEER

Have you ever talked to someone who has hit a deer with his car? Even though the situations may differ between individuals—"It was dark and he ran out in front of me" or "I went around the corner and he was just standing there"—no matter what the tale, they will all end with the same sentiment: "I had no idea it could do that much damage."

Deer are dense animals. They're upward of three hundred pounds of muscle and tissue and bone, and they eat healthy and exercise all day. And when you hit one in your car at thirty-five miles an hour, it'll put one heck of a dent in the thing. God forbid you hit one going any faster. I've heard of bumpers ripped off, windshields smashed, and hoods caved in. I have an uncle who swears that he hit a deer once and flipped his car completely over (of course, he's the type who might actually hit an already-dead carcass like a ramp just to see if he could get some air). I've even heard stories of deer flying through the windshields of cars and kicking people to death as they writhed through their own death. It's a thoroughly unpleasant thing, hitting a deer.

And if a deer can do that much damage to a car, can you imagine what it would do to a bicycle? I can tell you the answer to that one: not much at all. But the rider? He gets absolutely nuked.

I used to be quite an avid mountain biker. I enjoyed racing when I was much younger, and then I got married and complacent and fat. But then sometime around 2004, my wife suggested we get fit by participating in the Balance Bar Adventure Sprint. This is an event where you run over six miles, swim a mile and a half, kayak around a lake, ride your mountain bike across fifteen miles of terrain, and test your mettle in feats of strength and dexterity. It's what would happen if *Fear Factor* adopted a triathlon format.

To get ready, I would drive down to Dauset Trails Nature Center, home to one of the absolute best mountain bike trails in Georgia. I started lightly, going every weekend, and as I got faster and braver and the adrenaline junkie in me began to awaken, I started going every single night. I couldn't get enough of the steep hills, log jumps, ramps, and bridges—all in all, over fifty miles of excitement and adventure. But my favorite part of the entire trail was a short, extremely steep jump run called Pine Mountain.

I ran the Pine Mountain course at least three times every single night. I adored it. It started off at a high elevation with a gorgeous view of the nature preserve below. Once you started down, you reached twenty-five miles an hour extremely quickly, and then the jumps started. These earthen banks launched you straight outward while the ground below you sank ever farther, allowing you to catch major air. Given the steepness of the terrain and the speeds you were traveling, you had to keep your wits about you at all times. Flubbing a landing on any one of those jumps meant the difference between going home sweaty and going home bloody and/ or broken.

On one particular evening, I was going through my paces on the trail system and reached Pine Mountain just as the sun began to sink beneath the tree line. I knew I had only about thirty minutes of usable daylight left, and I had to make this one run count. With a full head of steam and all the confidence of a mountain biker who'd just crossed the line from amateur to "experienced," I pumped my legs as hard as I could to get rolling down the hill.

In no time, I was at my top speed of about twenty-five miles an hour, and when the jumps arrived, I began popping and landing them with the skill and finesse of a guy who thinks he has a lot of skill and finesse but really looks like a grown-up hopping molehills on his too-expensive bicycle. Just as I reached the first turn in the trail, a huge brown blob whipped in front of me and blocked my path.

There was no time to brake, or skid out, or try to bail off the bike and let it take the damage. I couldn't even brace for the impact; it just happened. It was like hitting a brick wall that was built waist-high. It hadn't even registered that the thing I'd hit might have been a mammal. All I really knew was that something brown had just stopped my wheels from moving and dislodged me from my mountain bike, and I was going to die wondering what the hell it was.

I hit the ground—*hard*. I was lucky as hell, because I'd hit the only finger of land that extended out to a much steeper decline down into the nature preserve. A foot to the right, and I'd have soared like Wile E. Coyote into the abyss. Good thing I didn't, because I hadn't packed my Uh-Oh sign in my CamelBak.

Like anyone does upon falling down, the first thing I did was attempt to move. A quick internal system check registered severe pains from my knee, abdomen, and right arm. Were they too severe to stand? Let's see . . . nope. I could get to my feet. My knee was cut, and my sock and shoe were soaked in blood. Any break? Doesn't seem so, just a minor flesh wound. Where the right arm was concerned, I knew immediately that I'd rebroken my wrist, because it felt like it had the last six times I'd broken it. As for the abdomen, every step I took and every breath I inhaled sent a shock up my body. It felt like someone had knocked the wind out of me and then kept punching me for fun.

I trudged over to my bike, which lay about twenty feet ahead of me. Once I got to it, I propped myself on it and surveyed the area for exactly what it was that I'd obliterated (there was no way in hell that anything could have survived the impact with the bullet my bike had become). Lying a few yards up the trail was the deer I'd hit.

Even in the fugue state I was in, I knew better than to walk up to a hulking mass of horns and hooves and attempt to awaken it. But I needed to know if it was still alive. I'd have felt horrible to have killed this poor thing just because

I wanted to go down a hill really fast. So I called out: "Hey, deer!"

No response except for the little bolt of pain from my side.

"Deer!" I continued. "Hey, deer! Wake up, deer!"

Nothing.

I winced a little as I reached for the strap of my Camel-Bak. Slowly, I removed the bag and brought it around to the front of me, so I could reach in for a PowerBar. With what little effort I could muster, I lobbed the carb-loaded food replacement bar at the animal. It landed on the deer's hind quarters with a lackluster *paff*.

No movement.

I hurled my full CamelBak at the thing. The weight of the water-filled bag hit the deer right in the head and startled it awake. It began lurching to its side, attempting to right itself, and once it got to its feet, it stared at me.

Which surprised me. I'd figured he'd get a glimpse of me and take off running. But I guessed these nature-preserve-raised animals weren't really scared of humans. He just looked at me, silently asking the question: "Dude, what the *fuck* was that?"

"Uh, sorry, deer," I said to him.

He just kept looking.

"You, uh, you okay?"

No response save for a small sway of the head and a shake of his antlers.

"You wanna, like, trade insurance information or anything?"

He stood there, staring.

I didn't know what to do. I was somewhat scared that the deer might try to charge me. But the sun was going down, and I'd run out of whatever patience one might possess that would allow him to stand in the middle of the woods with a bloody leg, a broken wrist, and fractured ribs and have a one-sided conversation with a deer. I abandoned the little chat I was having with Mr. Deer and let him keep my CamelBak. I began pushing my bike up the hill I'd descended, keeping one eye on the huge mammal I'd bludgeoned with a bicycle.

The entire time, he watched me walk up the hill. He didn't make any moves toward or away from me. He just kept his eyes on me. Every time I'd look back, he was standing there watching me limp up the hill with my bike. When I got to the top, I waved at him with my good hand and said, "Okay, later, deer. Get checked out by a doctor."

I failed to notice the two mountain bikers at the head of the Pine Mountain Trail who'd arrived in time to hear me talking to the animal. They took one look at me and said, "Holy shit, dude!"

"Yeah," I said, not even bothering to play tough. "I hit a deer."

"Fuck," one guy said.

"You want some help?" said the other.

Usually, when someone takes a fall or has a flat or whatever, someone else will pass by and offer help, knowing full well that the offer won't be taken up. I wanted to tough this one out and be a hero and make it to my car on my own, if for no other reason than to prove that I wasn't nearly as bad off as I felt. But the bolts of pain going through my body were telegraphing to my brain, saying, "Hey, dummy, you need some help." So I accepted their offer.

The bike had taken relatively little damage. The wheel and the handlebars had gotten twisted and turned sideways, which was a relatively easy fix, and I'd broken a reflector. I learned that there's very little you can do for a broken rib besides sit around and do nothing. But I also learned that dusk at a nature preserve is the wrong time to go testing the speed and handling capabilities of your mountain bike.

The recovery efforts from the accident put the kibosh on my mountain biking for a while, and I ended up selling the bike and turning to other endeavors, like eating a little too well and watching too much television. But I never lost the thirst for the speed and thrill of trees whizzing past and the sight of rapidly approaching earth as I descended from a great jump. I still hate deers, though.

CHAPTER 8

JUST HANGIN' AROUND

I yelled for help for almost ten minutes before finally getting the attention of a young couple making their way to
their car in the back of the parking lot.

"HEY! Hey, can you guys help me? *Please?*"

"What are you doing up there?" the man yelled, standing at a safe distance. I can't say that I blame him for keeping
some space between us—we'd only just met, and here I was
suspended on a twelve-foot fence, ensnared in barbed wire
and bleeding profusely. He had little to fear, though; all I
wanted was to get the fuck down.

"I'm trapped. I'm, uh, I'm hurt pretty bad. I really need
help. Can you go get someone? Please?"

"Yeah, um . . ."

He stood there in complete disbelief at the scene he had
stumbled upon. Here was a nice, upstanding young man
taking his best girl out for a nice meal at Chili's. He probably
figured a few hours of dull conversation and some South-
western egg rolls would get him at least a hummer that

evening, possibly even laid. I am certain that the last thing he expected—or wanted—to see right then was me caught on the fence, begging for help. Wide-eyed and completely in shock, he stood there, utterly useless. The girl by his side finally chimed in. "What are you doing up there?"

"It's a long story. Please, I'm bleeding badly here." I did not feel like going through the entire story with them, and seeing as how my white oxford shirt and khaki pants had become a wet crimson due to various leaks around my body, surely any rational human being would cease asking questions and run—right away—to get some assistance. These guys, however, needed some coaching.

"Does it matter?" I asked. "Can you just go get the manager or somebody? Please?"

Nothing. No response at all. The immediacy of the situation began to become more and more apparent as the barbs from the wire dug deeper and deeper into my thigh and calf. It was one hell of a predicament I had gotten myself into.

I had been working for tips making balloon animals in restaurants for almost nine months at that point. Being a balloon twister was an extremely fun job, one of my absolute favorites. The job was perfect for that time in my life. I couldn't do it now, of course—it's fine for an eighteen-year-old working his way through college, but it's extremely creepy when full-grown adults do it. I worked from six P.M. until ten on Friday, Saturday, and Sunday nights and made enough to pay for college and my extremely demanding girlfriend at the time, Mandy.

In case it hasn't been clear until now, this chick was a real masterwork. She made insane claims on both my time and my money, insisting on spending every waking moment with me at the various shopping malls and department stores scattered around Georgia. That's what made the balloon job so nice—I had no setup or cleanup duties, so getting out on time was no problem whatsoever, which meant I didn't have to hear her complain about my working late. And the customers were genuinely nice to me, which I sincerely needed at that point, given the caliber of girl I was dating.

The only downside to the job was the fact that sometimes very large parties with a ton of kids would come into the restaurant and demand to have me at their table the entire time. This wouldn't be so bad if they compensated me for all of my time there, since I might be at their table for an hour or more. These folks meant well, but as a group, they usually tipped about the same as one person at one table, somewhere around three to five bucks. They didn't understand that making giraffes and swords for twenty-five screaming kids who were popping the balloons as soon as they got them in their grubby little paws and demanding replacements for over an hour of my night was worth more than three lousy dollars. I quickly learned to make my way to the other side of the restaurant once I saw a group like that enter the building.

That night, there happened to be a group of about fifty—only half of whom were adults—who wandered in at about 9:55 P.M. I had wanted to leave right on time that evening due to the fact that the hot new must-see movie of the summer, *Titanic,* had just opened, and Mandy was demanding that we see it that night.

Her: All of my friends have seen it! I'm the only one who hasn't!

Me: Two strangers meet and fall in love on the *Titanic*? It looks pretty stupid.

Her: Well, I think it's sweet. I want to see how they meet and how they fall in love! I bet it's *romantic!*"

Me: I don't mean to spoil it for you, but in the end, the boat sinks.

Her: Oh, shut up. I don't know what I'm going to do if we don't see it this weekend!

Me: Your heart will go on.

Her: What?

Me: Nothing.

Missing *Titanic* meant putting up with Mandy's shit. Doing balloons for these kids definitely meant missing *Titanic*. This logical process brought me to a very clear conclusion.

I peered from across the restaurant at the group. I could see the adults pointing at the various tables I had already visited, telling the children that balloons in the shape of a puppy or kitty cat would soon be theirs.

"Like hell they will be," I said to myself. There was no way I was about to get shanghaied by this group of wide-eyed children and have to face the wrath of Mandy. I knew it would be impossible for me to make it through that horde of demanding six- to ten-year-olds without having to explain to them that I was leaving for the evening and didn't have time to make them balloons, subsequently becoming a gigantic bastard in the tales they would tell when they got older, and forcing them into a depraved psychosis where they took out a Kmart with homemade fertilizer bombs or beat senior citizens with baseball bats.

"There are only three other exits besides the front—the back exit and the two fire exits—but those have alarms on them," Mike explained to me. He had recently started working there as a server to make a few extra dollars on the weekends, and in his usual Eagle Scout way, he had mapped out the entire place in case of a fire or a hostage situation.

"Ooh, the back exit. That sounds promising," I replied.

"I don't think you can leave that way. The back gate is locked."

"So? Go unlock it."

"Dude, I don't have the key."

"Who does?"

"Eric."

I was screwed.

Eric was the manager of Chili's. Eric loved the attention that the balloons brought to his restaurant, but he hated me and the other balloon twisters with a passion. He had tried several times to teach his waitstaff how to make balloon animals, and he'd asked the balloon service to discontinue my services once he thought he had it all figured out. He called me the next week when a regular customer's child cried her eyes out due to the waiter's inability to craft a fire engine with an extending ladder, and I was back the next weekend as the balloon expert at Chili's.

"Can't you get the key from Eric?" I asked.

"Heh. You try."

I knew that was impossible. Eric wouldn't help me if his life depended on it. Alas, I had no other option. Humbly, I approached Eric and began to beg for release.

"Hey, Eric, open the back gate for me," I demanded.

"Why do you need me to do that?"

"I need to get out of here."

"Go out of the front exit, like a normal human being," he replied.

"I can't. It's completely packed with demanding children and parents who won't take no for an answer. I don't have time to make two hundred balloon animals. I need to go, like, now."

He sighed. "What the hell am I paying you guys for? You're supposed to entertain my customers. *All* of my customers, even the demanding children."

"My agreement is to stay until ten. It's ten-oh-one. I'm done."

He sighed. "God, you're lazy."

"Fine, I agree with you, I'm lazy," I said. "I also gotta go. Will you open the gate or not?"

He gave me a stern look that implied I should never ever ask him for any favors ever again. "Nope. That gate opens only after hours. You have to go out the front."

That was simply not an option. I couldn't face those kids and outright deny them the pleasure of a giraffe or unicorn. I was much better at slinking out and making them sad by not being there than I was at rejecting their innocent pleas for a pirate hat or motorcycle.

I waited until Eric went into the front of the store before I sneaked through the kitchen and out the back door
leading to the cage, an enclosure housing the garbage bins
and grease traps, formed by the building wall and three sides
of twelve-foot-tall chain-link fence with three layers of
barbed wire at the top that were angled outward to prevent
someone from climbing in from the outside.

I surveyed the area—the Dumpsters were far too large
and heavy to push over to the fence, and there were no other
stepping stools. My only recourse was to scale the fence and
bound up and over the barbed wire, falling a mere fourteen
feet to the other side. Compared to the prospect of twenty-
five angry children and a very angry Mandy, it seemed like a
cakewalk.

"It's not that far to the ground. The fence is really easy
to climb. This will be nothing," I said aloud, trying my best
to bolster my confidence. I extended my arms and wrapped
my fingers around a section of chain links, then placed my
right foot in one of the many holes in the fence and
propelled myself up. In hindsight, I have to say that my brain
hated my body and wanted it to die. That is the only explanation I have for making the decision to try to exit the
premises this way.

I scaled the fence in pretty short order. Once I got to
the top, I balanced myself on the precipice of the barrier
and began the task of moving my feet past the barbed wire.
My right hand was planted firmly on one of the support
beams that angled the barbed wire outward from the fence;
my right foot was posted in one of the uppermost holes in
the fence; my body faced down and almost parallel to the

ground. I got my left foot over pretty easily. My right took a great deal more effort, as I was supporting myself almost completely with my upper body.

My right shoelace was dangling a bit and snagged on the second tier of barbed wire. I tugged a little to free it, to no avail. I then jerked hard in an effort to dislodge it from the barb, which sent my right leg up and over the barbed wire. In the process, I lost my balance and landed almost full-bodied on the top of the fence. Gravity then kicked in, sliding me down the angled face created by the layers of barbed wire, back toward the inside of the cage.

Instinctively, I rolled to regain my balance, which thrust me toward the outside of the cage. In the process, my shirt and pants became tangled in the barbs. As I struggled to keep from falling, I reached out and grabbed the barbed wire with my left hand, impaling it. Gravity, all the while, has been undaunted in its task to bring me plummeting to the concrete below. I kicked my left foot back and caught myself in between the topmost and second layers of wire, wrapping my leg almost completely around the second layer and stopping my fall but firmly securing myself in its grasp.

With the weight of my right leg dangling over the wire, my body shifted in that direction, leaving my left foot hung in the wire. I began to fall outside of the cage and was saved from dashing myself on the asphalt by the stinging barbs of wire wrapped tightly around my left leg.

My left hand had been ripped open by the barb that had burrowed into it when I began slipping. My abdomen was cut pretty deeply from rolling from my belly to my back on the barbed wire while trying to catch myself, and my leg was in shambles from being tangled up in the wire. I just hung there upside down, caught by one leg on the fence behind Chili's, clothes torn to shreds, and bleeding from several open wounds. This brings us back to the adorable yet moronic couple happening upon and subsequently staring at my limp and helpless form dangling to and fro.

Struggling to make sense of the fact that they stood there motionless, watching someone in mortal peril begging for their assistance, I finally lost my temper. "Hey!" I yelled. "Are you going to help or not?"

I guess it's not proper etiquette to shout at total strangers when soliciting help from them, especially when you are entangled in the most notorious antitheft measure in the world and bleeding profusely. The guy decided against running into the restaurant to get help and instead pulled out his cell phone and dialed what I could only assume was 911. All I could hear of the following conversation was on our end. He was saying, "Some lunatic . . . barbed wire . . . Chili's . . . bleeding . . . angry . . . PROBABLY A THIEF." He listened for a moment, asked the person on the other end of the line to hold on, looked up at me, and yelled, "The police are on their way. Don't move."

I sighed. "Ha, ha, very funny. Where the hell am I going to go?"

He thought that over, then quickly brought the phone back to his ear, repeating to the operator on the other end exactly what I had said. I imagine she was probably coaching him on how to handle this situation as he ushered his woman toward their car and told her, "Wait here, I'll handle it." He listened to the next set of instructions, nodding periodically in response to whatever advice the operator was giving. I wanted to shout to him that the person he was talking to probably couldn't hear the nuts rattling inside his skull when he nodded, and that he would need to speak up a bit, but at that point, the world was turning purple and I was finding it harder and harder to pay attention to anything at all.

Time passed. Exactly how much, I am not sure, because I started slipping in and out of consciousness. Just as I settled into the inky blackness that surrounded and enveloped me, a very shrill wake-up call brought me to full attention. Three police cars, an ambulance, and a fire truck roared down the street and past my field of vision. I could see the red and blue lights reflecting on the trees and walls behind the building; I watched as the perspective of the lights shifted in response to the angles of the restaurant until they appeared directly in front of me. Several uniformed officers hopped out of their vehicles, guns drawn and trained on me. "Police! Don't move!"

This was fantastic. I stopped struggling so I could lift my head and see what was going on, then went limp and let my arms dangle, squinting against the bright spotlight. I thought, The only thing that could possibly suck more than this would be if it were in front of a whole lot of people who had exited the restaurant to investigate the goings-on outside of the fine eating establishment . . . Well, of all the luck. There they are now.

A huge crowd had formed to watch. There I hung and bled, spotlighted by the police and held at gunpoint. Amid the murmurs and gasps of my adoring public, I could hear a voice ringing true and loud—Mike was making his way forward to explain everything.

"Hey! This guy isn't a criminal, he's a balloon guy! Let me explain it to you! He works here!"

Eric shouted, "He does *not* work here! He's a *contractor*!"

Both Eric and Mike made their way to the police officers holding me at bay, because at any moment, I might sprout wings and fly away. A bit of conversation ensued, the result of which found the fire department on a ladder cutting me out of the barbed wire, to the applause of the onlookers, and the ambulance carting me off to the emergency room.

I wouldn't make it to see *Titanic* that night. And Mandy was so angry about that fact, she didn't even go with me to the emergency room. I suspect the rage she felt over missing the movie event of that summer contributed to her accusations of my homosexuality to my parents months later.

I was pretty bruised where my leg had been bound by the wire, and there were a few cuts here and there. The cuts on my left hand, inner left thigh, and abdomen were especially deep and required stitches—thirty-seven in all—each wound leaving a permanent reminder of exactly how stupid I am.

Explaining the entire scenario to the doctor stitching me up was a real pleasure. He had to stop the suturing several times as he broke out in hysterics at various parts of my tale. He eventually summoned several nurses standing near the main station outside of the room. "Hey! You guys gotta come hear this!" he exclaimed, asking me to restart my story once they'd entered the room.

Within a few minutes, I became the hit of the ER. Nurses and doctors showed up in pairs, then groups, then flocks to hear the verbal reenactment. I must have told and retold the story at least twelve times that evening. I was embarrassed at first but then grew comfortable with telling the tale to the ever-growing audience, knowing that my options were to either relate the story to them directly or let them hear a butchered secondhand account over a carton of milk and a cup of Jell-O in the staff cafeteria.

I didn't know until that day, but some doctors keep a running bet with their colleagues over what the oddest story each week will be. My actions had won my physician fifty bucks in the pool.

"Glad I could be of service, Doc. How about kicking a little of that my way, seeing as how balloon-animal making doesn't come with benefits?"

"Heh," he replied, then walked out of the door.

I instantly went from making a little over one hundred dollars that night, constructing parakeets and pandas out of colored latex, to spending half a grand on my deductible for the emergency room visit—all because I didn't have the stones to disappoint a bunch of kids or stand up to my bitch of a girlfriend. Oh, sneaking out was fine and dandy— disappointing people without having to look them in the eye is no problem whatsoever. After all, I had been doing it to my parents for years. However, place a puddle-eyed second grader hoping for a red and blue balloon ninja in front of me, or a psycho girlfriend, and instantly, I become a weak-willed jellyfish.

Mandy and I didn't get to see *Titanic* until the following weekend, and the entire time, she reminded me of how stupid I was for getting into the mess I'd gotten into.

> *Her:* See? This is the kind of crap you pull that ruins things for us! I just wanted us to have a nice night out!
>
> *Me:* I was climbing that fence for you, you silly bitch.
>
> *Her:* What did you just say?
>
> *Me:* Nothing.

CHAPTER 9

JUST VISITING

t really was great to see him again, even if it was from behind Plexiglas.

I took a long look at him as he situated himself in his chair. His long stringy black hair swayed across his neck as he rocked left and right, sliding the chair closer to the table before him. He looked almost exactly as he had when we were kids, with the notable exceptions of the goatee on his chin and upper lip and the tattoo on his chest, the top of which rose barely above the neckline of his T-shirt. It looked like it was probably a skull. He was also thinner and paler than I remembered.

"Jesus, Jason. Wow, man, it's . . ." I said. He looked up at me, a slight scowl adorning his face. I looked down at the table in front of me and shook my head slightly as I continued. "Wow. It's been a long time!" I looked back up at the man I hadn't seen in five years, and every day of our separation echoed in my voice. "How are you?"

Jason chose to respond by lighting a cigarette—slowly,

deliberately, allowing the act to effectively answer the question for him. It did, very loudly and very clearly.

Taking a slow, deep drag, he held the smoke deep in his lungs for several seconds. He stared into my eyes, holding my gaze until I broke and looked down at the table. I glanced back up at him in time to watch the side of his mouth crack a sly smile, allowing a thick fog to seep out slowly. He flicked into the small plastic cup sitting to his left the small chunk of ash that had formed at the tip of his cigarette, took another long look at me, and finally replied to me in a Southern accent that had grown more pronounced since I saw him last.

"Yeah, it has been a long time, you're right." His voice crackled and popped as he spoke, sounding almost mechanical and conditioned to respond when questioned. It then broke, revealing a flood of emotion as he blurted out, "Goddamn! Joe, man. It's damn good to see you, man! How you been?"

I exhaled the shallow pool of air I had been holding in my lungs, then allowed myself to take a deep breath, the first real breathing I had done since I had entered this building. "I can't really complain," I replied as casually as I could. "Work, school, you know. The typical shit."

He chuckled, drawing tiny circles on the table with his index finger. "Typical for you, maybe."

I blushed, embarrassed that I could be so absentminded as to forget his situation. The things that seemed typical to me had become distant visions for him, experienced through television screens and books and magazines. I didn't know

many felons, but I knew enough about the situation to realize that things like college and work and girlfriends were
seldom brought up in conversation here, and when they
were, they were discussed in the past or future tense.

"Oh. Wow, I'm sorry—"

"Don't be." He took another long drag from his cigarette.
After a short silence and a cloud of smoke blown from his lips,
he spoke again. "You pretty much know what I'm doing.
How about you tell me what you're doing now, man."

It took a moment for me to think about the things I was
doing each and every day. I was trying to find a way to tell
him about my daily rituals without rubbing them in his face.
"During the day, I work in the computer lab at school."

He looked moderately surprised. "No shit! Graduated
and turned college boy, huh? Where you goin', Clayton
State?"

"No, Georgia State, actually."

"Oh, yeah, that one." He furrowed his brow and asked,
"That the one down there, down in Statesboro?"

"No, no, that's Georgia Southern. State is downtown."

"Oh." Another drag, another silence, another minute
ticked by. "So, computers, huh?"

I shifted in my seat. "Yeah, it's pretty boring. Mostly, I
just listen to a bunch of students bitch about the printers not
working."

"Sounds like fun," he said sarcastically. I noticed that as his
hand lay on the table, it was shaking. He saw me looking at it
and smiled a little. "But them computers, that's right up your
alley, huh? You always liked playin' those games and stuff."

"Yeah, helping a bunch of whiny English majors who cry because they can't figure anything out for themselves. It's real fun."

He laughed. "You just say that because you'd rather be playing them video games!" With a raspy mixture of coughing and laughing, he added, "Am I right?" He smiled, revealing a mouthful of nicotine-stained teeth.

I laughed a little. "Yeah, they don't really let me do that while I work. Gotta 'earn' that minimum wage, you know?"

"Beats being here," he said, gesturing at the back of the building.

I cleared my throat, embarrassed again. Forgoing yet another apology, I went on telling him about my life. "At night, on the weekends, I make balloon animals for kids in a restaurant."

He cocked his head a little to the left. "You're a clown?"

"No no no, not a clown. I wear normal clothes and all. I make the balloon animals for tips. Not a clown, just a guy who, you know, makes stuff. Out of balloons."

"Heh." He snorted, not buying a word of it. "Hey, you ever make anything like a big dick or something?"

I laughed. "Naw, man . . . of course not! These are for kids!"

"So?" He had a gigantic grin on his face, the one he always had when he was being a jackass. His statement was fantastically funny, so deadpan and so typical of his character. I wanted to laugh. Instead, all I could think about was how he should have been at graduation with Mike and me, and how he should have been going to college with us, and how unfair life had been to him.

I began to cry.

He shook his head violently and knocked on the glass between us. "Hey, man, you gotta stop that shit. I'm not about to sit here and watch that."

He was right. Remembering where I was and how long I had with him, I steeled myself, wiping away the small streams that the tears had formed on the sides of my face. "I'm sorry, man. It's just that, you know . . ."

"Yeah, I know." He stared at the table in front of him, elbows resting on top of it, hands clasped in front of his nose. A thin stream of smoke emanated from the tip of the cigarette he clutched between his yellowed fingers; it drifted toward the ceiling in an almost perfectly straight line. He looked back up at me, and in an obvious effort to bring a little levity to the situation, he began to reminisce.

"Hey, yo . . . you remember that class we had to go to, that one we had to take after we shot up those trucks with that slingshot? You and me and . . . that kid, the skateboarder . . . what's his name . . ."

"Mike," I said, wiping my eyes once more.

"Yeah, that guy . . . Mike. You still talk to him?"

"Yeah. He's my roommate now."

"Oh, you out of the folks' place?" He flicked a bit of ash into the ashtray.

"Yeah, we share a house with my sister's fiancé, over near Mount Zion."

His eyes grew wide. "Whoa, Jenny? She's gettin' married?"

"Yeah."

"Wow, that's crazy! She sure grew up, huh?" He looked

at the wall to his left and then cut quickly back to the right, pounding the cigarette-free hand against the table as he exclaimed, "Damn! You know, man, everybody's movin' on. It's . . ." His face relaxed slightly and his eyes softened a bit. "It's good, though, you know? It's real good."

I nodded.

He sat silent, then continued. "Anyway, one of the kids that was in that class, that juvenile delinquent class . . . he's on my block. Omar, the kid who took the jewelry from Parisian. You remember that kid?"

I didn't know who the hell he was talking about. I remembered the class and how scared Mike and Jason and I had been in it, sitting in and among thieves and hooligans who had beaten people with sticks and shovels—one girl had beaten her mom with a lamp. Still, I went with it; it was far better than silence or sniveling like a child from the other side of the window. "What did he do to end up here?" I asked.

Jason smashed the butt of his cigarette into the ashtray with his right hand, simultaneously grabbing the pack that sat in front of him with his left and shaking out a new one. He positioned the red-and-white package in front of his face and yanked out a new smoke with his lips. With the cigarette clinging to his mouth, he answered, "Manslaughter. Shot up his old man, put two in his face."

I sat there as Jason lazily dragged the head of a match against the back of a book. He quickly brought the lit match to the tip of his cigarette, causing the small cylinder to glow red and smoke furiously, mimicking what was happening to my brain as I searched for the words to say next. Nothing came readily to mind, and all I could do was try to imagine what it would take to get me mad enough to "put two" into the face—or any other body part—of a person. I didn't know Omar's circumstances, and I wasn't sure what a person needed to have inside himself to get to the point of shooting someone, much less his father. I had done—and probably would do in the future—some pretty questionable things in my life, yet one thing I was reasonably certain of was that I lacked whatever it took to kill someone.

Jason coughed, bringing my attention back to him. It was clear that current events weren't something that we could find a common ground on, so I sprinted as fast as I could back toward memory lane. "Hey, you remember that stupid kid Todd?"

"The one I lived next to?" he said, lazily drawing in smoke from his Marlboro. "The one you traded the porno tapes with and got you caught by your mom?"

"Wait, what do you mean, I traded with?" I asked with a grin. "Man, *you* made that trade on my behalf!"

"Hey, don't pin that shit on me, motherfucker," he said with a smile as he pounded his chest with two fingers. "You didn't have to cough up that tape . . . you could have said no!"

"You know, I never even got to watch the damn thing. Well, actually, I did . . ."

"Yeah, I remember you telling me about that!" he said, laughing loudly. "I would have *loved* to see that shit in person.

You in the living room with your mom and pops while two girls are dykin' it out on the TV . . . The look on your mom's face would be worth at least a million bucks!" He drifted off a bit, then returned with "Say, how is your mom, anyways?"

"She's not bad. You know, same ol' Mom. She asked me to tell you hi. And my dad, well . . . you know my dad. Always on my back about something. In fact, I just bought this car, and—"

"Did he ever forgive you for when we blew up that art desk trying to make our own firecrackers?" he interjected, obviously uninterested in any conversation about a car.

"I think he thought it was pretty funny," I said, a bit stunned by the interruption. "I ended up having to buy a new one, though."

We chuckled a bit as we remembered that incident and so many others that had made us best friends as children. Another short silence situated itself directly between us, personifying the severe discomfort that accompanies a conversation through a speaker in a window at Lovejoy—or any correctional facility, for that matter. The deafening lack of noise became unbearable, apparently for both of us. Jason's eyebrows raised, and he hacked out a smoker's cough as he pointed at me. "You know who I always wonder about?"

"Who's that?"

"That punk motherfucker John Dixon. Man, I'd like to beat his ass."

The name hit me like a cinder block.

"Jesus . . . wow. John Dixon," I whispered as a chaotic swarm of thoughts and feelings swept through me. It was impossible to pin down one emotion to feel, as everything ranging from anger, to remorse, to severe depression made its way through my gut. I lifted my head to look at a broken, incarcerated man sitting on the other side of a thick pane of Plexiglas, clad in orange, manacles and handcuffs adorning his ankles and wrists. All I could see, however, was the goofy comic-collecting kid who had lived up the street from me. Once he was my best friend in the world. This was the guy who had introduced me to heavy metal (the music) and *Heavy Metal* (the movie), a kid who had stood by my side through thick and thin—the thickest of which was the night he received a punishment he shouldn't have because of a cowardly asshole named John Dixon.

It was almost five years before, over Christmas vacation during our freshman year in high school. The bright glow of moonlight diffused through thick clouds turned the sky a bright purple, illuminating slightly the meeting spot of a particularly mischievous trio of young men. A trio whom my mom had unwittingly dubbed "a scourge upon this subdivision" after viewing an unsigned blue, green, and gold scrawl painted on the driveway of one of our neighbors, suggesting he "suck a cock." She had no idea that any of the three of us was involved. She just knew that whoever had vandalized such a nice neighbor's driveway was "a plague" and she "hoped he was soon caught." First a scourge, then a plague! I felt truly honored.

Jason and I were at the meeting spot, making preparations for the evening's activities, accompanied by our partner in crime, John Dixon. John was a six-foot-five lanky boy one year our elder, brushing his windswept hair from his eyes as he explained with a guilty smirk that there was no way on earth we would ever get caught.

"Dudes, we are too good at this!" he said with the oratory skill of a politician. "We've never been caught before, right? Besides, we didn't get pictures of the car lot. We need them!"

"Dude," Jason said, exasperated from having argued this point for the past twenty minutes, "we just did that place last week! We can't go back there, not so soon." He was finishing a bottle of Michelob he had stolen out of his father's secret refrigerator in the toolshed, the one we were conspiring behind. He offered me the rest, but I waved it off as I arranged the harness I had just fastened around my waist. Jason shrugged, swigged the last of the bottle, and offered that we "do the library."

"The library?" John asked. "The library isn't any kind of challenge. Kids do that place all the time. I'm telling you, we need to get the car lot again!"

I hooked the hammer Jason had handed me into the small loop on the side of the belt I had gotten perfectly situated around my hips and said, "Look, let's just decide on a place. I don't care where, I just wanna fuck something up tonight."

John stood his ground. "The car lot. We gotta get the lot. More targets, and it's the only place we don't have pictures of yet."

Jason sighed, preparing to argue the point again, when I interjected, "Fine," tired of lollygagging. "The car lot. Let's just get going. It's almost three, and I gotta get up at six to work on the house with my dad." I hoisted the canvas drawstring bag filled with the tools of our particular trade and slung it over my shoulder. It always fell on me to carry the gear, since I was the strongest and most capable of being the mule of our little group. A mile and a half with a bag and a tool belt would have made Jason collapse, and John had his hands full with the cameras.

"Man, I dunno," Jason offered once again as he began following John and me across his backyard and up to the road.

"Jason, dude, just shut up! Let's get this thing GOING!" John exclaimed.

Jason's concern was quickly abandoned as we trotted along in our black hooded sweatshirts and black cargo pants, singing in gasps and whispers marching cadences that John's brother sent him from the marines. The cadence fell in time with the slapping of our Hi-Tec boots against the wet asphalt. I was watching my breath come out in small billows of steam with each step, inhaling deep the moist December air as the canvas bag over my shoulder pounded against my back, and the hammer and crowbar hanging on either side of the harness around my waist tapped lightly against each leg.

Winding through the roads of our neighborhood and cutting across the dark wooded back lot of the apartments at the northern edge of the subdivision, we took up position behind some bushes as we considered the rental car lot located directly across the street from our neighborhood. The lot housed a fleet of ghost-white rental vans, trucks, and cars—each and every one an unmarked canvas for the "art" we were about to so proudly practice.

"Look! It's a whole new batch!" John said. He looked at Jason and said, "See. I told you this was the place to be tonight!"

Jason was nearly salivating as I plopped the bag on the moist ground and pulled the strings open. "You were *so* right," Jason said to John, reaching into the bag and grabbing a large pair of bolt cutters. "Man, this rules! Look!" He pointed toward the back of the lot at the dense kudzu climbing the fence he would cut open with the implement he wielded in both hands. "They barely even patched the fence! It's barely holding together, I can see the hole from here!" He laughed as he began to head over from behind the apartment building.

I reached into the bag and grabbed several cans of Krylon spray paint, handing John his trademark green and stuffing Jason's red and my gold into the side pockets of my pants. Leaving the bag behind, the three of us quickly and silently moved up along the side of the building, sprinted across the street, and slid behind the fence, burying ourselves in the thick kudzu vines as the entire structure rattled and waved. It was completely dark, with the exception of the moonlit clouds high in the sky. My heart was racing from the thrill, my gut churning and adrenaline pumping. It was times like these that made me—and my companions—feel alive. I smiled at Jason, who went to work snipping open the small staples that held together the severed links of the fence we had cut open a week ago.

As Jason finished clamping the jaws of the bolt cutters on the last band of metal at the top of the flopping fence, John tapped him and pulled him back against the loose foliage. Raising his finger to his lips and giving the universal "shhhh!" sign, he squatted, and we followed suit. Just then a truck inside the lot very slowly proceeded down the horizontal row farthest from us.

Thrill turned into terror as my heart nearly stopped and my breathing ceased. We watched the truck drive slowly past each row. The headlights were off and the engine was kept to a low rumble as the driver stealthily patrolled the lot that had been vandalized the week before. The truck rolled toward our row, then past it without pausing. We thought we were out of the woods. But then it crept to a stop just past the row we were staring down. From behind the fence we could barely see the passenger door slowly creak open. A crouched form made its way out of the vehicle. A final puff of exhaust exited the tailpipe as the driver shut off the engine and joined his companion, meeting him around the front of the vehicle.

"Oh, *shit,*" I heard John whisper. Jason kicked him, causing the leaves around his leg to rustle slightly but audibly.

The men on the other side of the fence paused and took up position behind the last car on the row where we were poised to enter the lot. I felt John's left hand extend behind him to my leg, and I saw his right hand stretch forward to rest on Jason's shoulder. He tapped once lightly, counting in a whisper, "Three . . ."

My heart began to race, pounding in my ears. I could no longer hear anything; I merely felt the whisper echo through the air as John tapped my leg and Jason's shoulder once more and muttered, "Two."

A final tap landed on the inside of my right thigh, and the air broke as John shouted, "ONE!"

The scene became pure chaos. Acting on instinct, the three of us bolted through the kudzu, racing along the edge of the fence and onto the street. Our advancement was mirrored on the other side of the fence by the two figures stalking us, held up momentarily by the gate they had to fling open. Out of the corner of my eye, I saw Jason turning left, racing back toward our neighborhood. He would be safe; the subdivision was rife with hiding spots. John turned right and sprinted toward the main highway, which was rich with gas stations and small shops he could duck behind, in, or under. I continued straight toward the apartment complex we had crept through not ten minutes before.

My pounding heart paused in response to a gunshot, followed by another and another behind me. They were followed by loud shouting and commands to "halt!" and "stop where you are!" Given that they never identified themselves as cops, and the truck they were in wasn't police-issue, I wasn't interested in complying. My legs churned and the tools on my hips flew about, accompanied by the rattle of the small balls inside the cans of spray paint.

I don't know how I became aware of it, as I couldn't hear anything. It was more of a feeling, a presence behind me—somehow I knew that there was someone following me. I ran as fast as I could, kicking one leg in front of me as quickly as I could push off with the other. The man behind me did the same, his footsteps echoing behind me louder and louder.

He was gaining on me.

I came to the small hill directly in front of the apartment complex, moist with condensation and freshly mowed. The second my boot made contact with the grass, I lost my footing. My right leg kicked out in front of me as I landed on my hip, and I slid down the hill. I managed to make it to my feet as I came to the base of the short but steep hill and again began churning my legs as fast as they would go. The man behind me wasn't nearly as clumsy as I was—unfortunately for him, as my slide was much faster than his cautious descent.

I took half a second to look behind me and check his position; it was still way too close for comfort. I turned forward again, pumping my legs as hard as I could when I reached the asphalt parking lot behind a row of buildings. My mind was in overdrive, but nothing coherent was happening in my brain as I brought myself closer and closer to a Dumpster nearly blocking the alley I was running through. There was a slight gap between it and the building, and I began calculating just how much time it would take me to make it through. Fortunately, I spotted a gift from God Himself: a worn-out and discarded love seat.

I bounded off the ground, placing my boot on the cushion of the love seat. I was trampolined up and on top of the garbage bin, clambered across it, and plopped to the ground on the other side. It wasn't graceful, but it worked. I resumed sprinting.

I turned down one of the rows of buildings and spotted in front of me a small wooden door near the steps of the building to my left. I flung it open, dove inside, and closed it behind me. I gathered myself into a ball and held my breath, swearing an oath to God that I would never, ever again sneak out of my parents' house at night, vandalize anything, steal anything, think dirty thoughts, or sneeze during church if She would just *please* get me out of this one.

I sat silently in the red Georgia clay beneath the apartments for what felt like an eternity, waiting for my pursuer to find me. It took minutes to catch my breath in the musty air, but slowly, I began to calm down. My heart rate dropped, and complete thoughts began to organize in my head—the first of which was: I've gotta find John and Jason. I cautiously crawled back over to the small door that led to the outside world (and much fresher air). I cracked it open, peeking out to see what I could see, which turned out to be absolutely nothing. I crouched in a ready position, and on my own count of three, I swung it open and leaped out, rolled, and came to my feet, ready to break into a sprint if someone was waiting to apprehend me. Nobody was.

I scanned the immediate area, looking for any sign of anything remotely recognizable or interesting. The only thing that made itself apparent was the canvas bag, which sat in a lump about thirty yards to my left behind the last building in the row where we'd prepared ourselves. I jogged over to it, and with each step, I realized that the cans of paint in my cargo pockets were rattling. No wonder the man had been able to follow me for so long. I grabbed up the bag and emptied my belt and pockets into it.

How on earth am I going to find them? I thought. God answered in the form of a panicked and extremely loud whisper from behind a house to the right of the apartment complex. It was Jason, waving his arms and signaling me to make my way over to him.

"Have you seen John?" he asked as I dropped the bag in front of him and ducked behind the hedgerow.

"No, you?" I replied, catching my breath from the sprint.

"No," he replied. "Holy shit, man! Those guys had a gun! They were shooting at us!" He dropped the bolt cutters into the bag.

"Yeah . . . Oh, man. John . . ." I said, expelling gigantic clouds of fog as I huffed. "I hope he didn't get shot!"

Jason shook his head. "Man, what the *hell* are we going to do? He probably got picked up. He's probably *dead!*"

"Just calm down!" I commanded. "Remember the contingency plan? He's probably behind your house waiting for us. We gotta get back there."

"Yeah, you're right. Let's get back there," he agreed.

We began to run back to Jason's house, this time sans marine cadence. All thoughts of jovial camaraderie turned to concern for our missing friend as we approached Jason's shed without a single trace of John anywhere to be found.

The word "shit" was said many, many times during the ensuing search for our third member. During the next few hours, Jason stuck by my side as we looked all around his house, my house, the filling stations that littered the main highway, the apartment complex, the scene of the crime. There was nowhere we didn't look, and every single place we searched turned up no sign of John. I finally offered the only plan that made sense to me: "We gotta call the cops."

"Are you *crazy*?" Jason asked, knowing full well that I was. "We'll get caught!"

"It doesn't matter, man," I said as the sun began to

lighten the eastern sky. "If he's been caught, we all go down together—we leave no man behind, remember?" Our borrowed code of ethics from John's brother the marine filled Jason's heart as he slowly nodded in agreement. We trotted as quickly as we could to my house, sneaked in, and dialed up the local police department.

"Clayton County Police," the officer said as brightly and cheerfully as you can imagine a policeman working the graveyard shift would.

"Uh, hi," I said. My heart was pounding, causing my voice to quiver. "I was wondering if you guys have a friend of mine in—"

"Name?"

"Uh . . . John Dixon."

A small silence, a deep breath, and the reply: "Nope. No one by that name has been brought in."

"Are you su—"

"Yes, very sure."

"Um . . . Okay, thank you—"

A resounding click echoed through the earpiece.

"Don't got him?" Jason asked. He was shaking as badly as I was. I shook my head. "So what do we do now?" he said, pleading, completely giving up.

"There's only one thing left," I said gravely. "We tell our parents."

He stopped shaking. He looked me square in the eye. "Fuck you."

"Dude, we don't have a choice," I said as he resumed shivering. "We gotta tell 'em!"

He shook his head. "You tell your parents, they tell

mine, and my ass is hamburger!" he said with panic in his voice. "It's not an option!"

"Dude, I swear, I'll tell them it was just John and me. I won't even mention your name."

"Don't. Seriously, man," Jason replied. "It'll come out somehow, and my dad will kick the shit out of me. You know he will."

Our conversation was halted by a small chirp of a ring from the phone. It didn't even make it through a full ring before falling silent. With the hopeful mind of a young teen, I began thinking of all the reasons that might have been . . . wrong number, surge on the phone line, ghost in the machine . . .

A short while later, the door to my bedroom opened to reveal my father in his nightshirt, staring holes through the pair of us. My mother, clad in her terry-cloth bathrobe, was standing right behind him. They wore an expression that revealed they knew far more than we had intended to tell them—and they were going to kill us because of it.

"John's mother just called here," my mother said through her scowl. I swear to God, her eyes glowed red.

Those five words spoke volumes about our current situation. Not only was John all right, but he had spilled the beans about the entire evening to his parents, who, in turn, had called my parents. But his version of the story was slightly different from ours. We found out through my mother—at very high volume—that John had decided we weren't the right kind of friends for him and "had made a break for it" moments before Jason and I could "force him against his will to vandalize the car lot."

Our ringleader had sold us out.

I was incredulous. I wanted to set the story straight. "I'll have you know—"

My father cast a Cone of Silence with his rage. "I am NOT interested in the slightest in anything you might have to say!" he exclaimed in a voice that would melt steel. "John told us what you were going to make him do to those cars!"

My mother chimed in merrily, "Jason, honey, you'd better get home. Your father's waiting for you." Before he could even respond, she added, "Oh, yes, he knows all about it! He was on a three-way call with us. You're in big trouble, too, mister!"

Jason just sat there. Slowly, tears began to wash across his face. He stood up, excused himself past my parents, and left my house. I stared at the floor and prepared myself for the devastation.

The tan of the worn carpet in my old bedroom room gave way to the white cold tile of a penal institution as I was startled back into reality by a sharp rapping against the Plexiglas window that separated me from the inmate on the other side of it.

"Yo!" Jason shouted through the speaker. "Wake up."

My eyes shot toward him as I attempted to collect myself. "I'm sorry," I answered. I had been absorbed by my little trip into the past for over a minute. I guessed Jason had gotten sick of hearing himself breathe. "That name just brought back some memories."

He nodded. "It does the same to me. I hate that motherfucker for turning on us like that. He got my ass *kicked* that night." He took a drag from his cigarette and added, "My old man took a damn fire poker to my hide."

"Yeah, my parents hit the roof, too," I replied glibly, knowing very well that my punishment of "lots and lots of chores" to pay off the vandalism couldn't possibly compare to what Jason had suffered. I knew Jason's dad, and "fire poker" wasn't a metaphor for anything. "I don't know what happened to John," I continued. "I didn't talk to him at all after that night. He never would face us."

"Joe, man," he said in a different tone, one that almost sounded like the Jason I grew up with. "Thanks for coming down here. I know this ain't easy, doing this here thing. I mean, I *gotta* be here, you know? You don't." His voice had become more gruff. He spoke more simply, and when he did, he sounded bitter and worn. But he was still Jason. He still had stuck by me when I got my ass kicked in elementary school. He had been there when I was jumped in the bathroom by six other kids in junior high. He had searched the neighborhood for our traitorous friend after our vandalism took a turn for the worst.

I looked at him in earnest. "Yeah, man, of course. What are friends for, right?"

He scoffed. "You're the only one of my 'friends' been down here. Ain't nobody wanna be your friend when you've been locked up for holding up a bank." He lit a new cigarette between his lips, cupping his hand over his mouth as he spoke. "To be honest, I didn't even think you would show, since you never answered my damn letters. Surprised the shit out of me when they told me you was here."

I sighed heavily, not knowing what to say. The absolute truth was that I didn't want to be there—no one in his right mind would. I hadn't seen him in over five years, since the summer after our freshman year in high shool, when he went off to an "alternative school." We were so different now—a difference made clear by the Plexiglas separating us. Two guys from similar backgrounds. Childhood friends who had chosen different paths in life: one who learned from his mistakes, graduated from high school, and went on to college (albeit for only a year); and one who attempted to liberate a bank of its holdings and was arrested and sentenced to ten years in prison. I guess home life goes a long way toward individual development. While my father never understood anything I was into, at least he didn't beat the hell out of me for being into it.

I didn't even know why Jason had written to me. I could only surmise that he had reached a point of loneliness where he decided to send out letters, writing to anyone and everyone he possibly could. Even more puzzling was the reason I was there: I didn't have one. Not one I could put into words, anyway. Perhaps it was curiosity, the desire to see how much of the Jason I once knew still existed. Maybe it was boredom—I had nothing to do that afternoon, and Lovejoy was only fifteen miles away. But if I didn't want to be there, why was I?

We sat in silence for another few minutes, each of us unsure what to talk about next. Had I known how long we had left, I would have thought of something else to say. Unfortunately, the buzzer sounded, marking the end of our twenty minutes. A correctional officer appeared beside Jason, tapping him on the shoulder and instructing him to head back to his cell.

He knew as well as I did that this would be my only visit. I tried to say goodbye, but nothing came out. I just looked at him looking at me, devoid of emotion, blank as slate. He met my gaze and said, "Stay good out there, man."

I nodded as he turned to waddle away in his chains. As he exited through the door that led to the cells, the reason I had shown up made itself clear: loyalty. As kids, we had faced entire classrooms full of jeers and taunts together. We'd been beaten up by the same bullies. We'd been friends when neither of us had friends, and that counted for a lot. That was Jason I'd just seen leaving. No matter what had happened or what he'd done, he was Jason.

I rose from my chair and headed out the doors. I felt myself walking faster and faster as I approached my car. I wanted out of there, badly. I slung open the car door and jammed my keys into the ignition, and as the engine turned over, the wave that had been building inside washed completely over me. There I sat outside the jailhouse, just visiting, unable to control myself as I lay my head on the steering wheel of my car and cried.

CHAPTER 10

OOOH, BURNED!

"I dunno," I said, plodding along the trodden path along-side Hwy 19-41, the main road through our city. I kicked a small hunk of quartz from the worn red clay path, used by carless people, into the flow of traffic, where it got crushed under the tire of a passing car. "I think DeLane's kinda cute."

"Kinda cute?" Mike replied, taking a swig from his quart-size bottle of Dr Pepper. He drew in a large breath, paused, and then released a huge, primitive belch.

"Eh," I replied, taking a gulp from my own drink, a bottle of Jolt cola. "She's all right. Nothing special."

"I'd do her," he said.

"You'd do anyone," I replied.

"Yeah, you're pretty much right." He kicked a rock of his own into the road, where it, too, met its demise under the tires of a passing vehicle. This was what there was to do in my town when you were sixteen and without any sort of vehicle. You walked to stores, kicked rocks into the road, and talked about girls.

I took a moment to enjoy the wind created by the passing traffic. The breeze from the cars and trucks roaring past us felt great in comparison to the stagnant oven of my bedroom. It was the hottest (and driest) summer at that point in Georgia history, and my parents couldn't afford to get the air-conditioning fixed. So Mike and I looked for any reason to get out of the house and go for a walk—especially when it would end up at an air-conditioned place. Mike's house was too far of a walk, as was the mall. But the brand-new Target was only three miles up the road, chock-full of sodas and candy and toys to play with and clerks to get mad at us, making it the perfect choice for our teenage rabble-rousing.

"So who would you pick?" Mike continued as we reached a crosswalk.

"I dunno," I answered. "Nobody in our school."

"Nobody?" he asked. "You wouldn't bang any of the girls in our class?"

I gave him a look. "Definitely not the ones in our class. Maybe one or two of the seniors or juniors . . . I dunno. But definitely not in our class."

"What about the fresh meat?" he asked with a smile, referring to the freshmen.

"Are you stupid?" I asked him.

"Yeah, why?" he answered.

I laughed. "You have to be to ask that question."

"It's a fair question," he replied. "Some of those younger chicks are hot."

"I dunno, man," I said as we crossed the driveway into a second-rate video store. "It seems to be the trend that as the years go by, the new girls get uglier and uglier."

"Ugly girls need love, too, you know." In nearly the same breath, he asked, "What about the girls working there?" He pointed at a skeleton of a building: the framework of the brand-new Hooters that was being built across the highway. Its road sign was already functioning, serving as a glowing orange beacon to all of the lads of our area that soon enough, a scantily clad woman would serve them horrible food in exchange for tips.

"Fuck, no," I said.

"Dude . . ." he said, stopping in his tracks to look at me.

"What?" I said, pausing to see what the hell he wanted.

"Dude, seriously . . . if you're gay, you can tell me."

I shook my head and began walking once again.

"No, I'm not kidding. You can tell me, I won't be mad," he said as he raised his soda to his lips.

"I'm not gay," I answered. "I just don't want to catch some sort of virus and have my thing fall off."

"Then wear protection!" he replied. "Wrap it, slap it, jam it in!"

"Do you even know what the hell you're talking about?"

He considered. "No, not really," he answered.

"Yeah, that's what I thought." I proceeded to swallow the last of my Jolt. "I'm out," I said, shaking my bottle.

"Yeah, me, too," Mike said, holding up his bottle to ensure that what he'd just said was correct. "Wanna stop now to get more, or hold out until Target?"

"Eh, we have another mile or so. Let's stop at that gas station," I replied.

We walked into the store and were greeted by the frosty chill of the air vent above the door. We stood there, fixed by the shift in temperature and our need to relish it. After a few moments of enjoying the cold, refreshing air, we made our way to the drink coolers to grab a bottle of our favorite tasty beverage.

"You got me on this one?" I asked.

He huffed. "I got the last one! This makes, like, the fifth time you borrowed money from me!"

"Yeah, I know," I replied with a shrug. "Get me on this one?"

He sighed and nodded. Again.

We were approaching the counter so Mike could pay for our drinks when I spied, with my little eye, a small basket next to the caffeine pills. It was full of matchbooks. As every adolescent boy is wont to do, I grabbed a handful and stuffed them into the pocket of my corduroy shorts. It was almost a matter of reflex: In much the same way you would swat a fly that buzzed past your nose, or scratch an itch on your leg, I saw matches and stuffed them into my pants. Matches are instant entertainment to a pair of teenage boys. At that age and in that town, it was easy to get bored.

We exited the store and marched on to Target, and on the way, we played this stupid game that Mike came up with that he called Flick. In Flick, you take a match from a matchbook, and then you wrap the cover of the matchbook over backward so that it touches the strike strip on the back. You place the match between the cover and the strike strip, then hold the entire ensemble over your head with your striking hand facing out. In one quick motion, you pull the match from between the cover and the back of the match-book, setting it alight, and flick it as far as you can. The match flares up in the air, allowing you to see where it lands (it usually flickers right out). Harmless fun for all.

There are no points in Flick, so there is no point to even play except that you get to see fire fly through the air. But when you're fifteen years old and walking three or so miles to hang out at a Target on a hot July night, you'll take anything that allows you to forget the repetition of monotony that comprises your life.

We arrived at the store and proceeded to wreak havoc on the place, like we always did. The second we entered the sliding doors, Mike took his place in one of the complimentary wheelchairs provided by the store, and I took my place behind him. I pushed him through the store at breakneck speed to the toy aisle, where we started opening the Nickelodeon Gak, wadding it into tiny balls, and throwing it up to the drop ceiling above, where it became permanently stuck (along with several hundred similar-looking wads placed there by us). It's nearly impossible to clean a thirty-foot ceiling. We then made our way to the video-game aisle to daydream about the electronic entertainment we couldn't afford, which was followed by a trip through the women's undergarments to don bras on our heads before buying ICEEs and hot dogs at the concession counter.

With our Freon-cooled Target Terrorism Mission complete, we left carrying our flavored-ice treats and hot dogs to begin the long walk home. We took turns alternating who would hold the drinks and who would play Flick. The whole time we discussed girls with whom we had no prayer of so much as getting a solid whiff of their hair, much less a chance at first base. I'd hold the drinks and talk about recently graduated senior Jennifer St. Claire while Mike flipped a lit match far ahead of us, and we'd walk right past the snuffed and smoldering strip of cardboard as we swapped places, then I'd take my turn while he daydreamed about Missy Staum (or Amanda Hyde, or Jennifer Dickenson, or . . .).

I don't remember whose turn it was when we flicked the match that hit the straw covering the newly seeded dirt around the Hooters construction area. All I can remember is thinking that this match, like all the others, would go out, and I remember walking by it exactly the same way we had the previous matches. I don't remember what the hell it was that made me turn around and check to see if it had gone out. It was a tiny whisper in the back of my mind: "Joe . . . look behind you . . ."

When I did, I was completely speechless. I dropped my ICEE cup and stared at the small bonfire that had formed not fifty yards behind us. Mike kept walking, and when he realized I wasn't beside him, he turned to check out why. I heard him yell from behind me something that sounded like "*Holy shit!*" He trotted up alongside me and asked the very question I'd had on my mind from the moment I laid eyes on it: "Did we do that?"

"Uh . . ." I said, watching the fire grow bigger literally by the second. "Yeah, I think we did." Apparently, extremely dry summers have an effect on straw and hay that, for some reason, fosters the spread of flame and fire. Unfortunately, we were merely sophomores and hadn't covered that part of science in our classes.

In the time it took us to share those stunned words, things went from bad to way worse. Almost as if God had reached down and moved the fire, it spread to a pile of lumber and roofing materials sitting a few feet away from the origin. It took only seconds for this pile to become engulfed. The glow of the fire was outshining the Hooters sign by nearly an order of magnitude. I believe that was when we decided it would be in our best interest to get the fuck out of there.

Without even saying a word, we turned on our heels and began hoofing it. I ignored the cramp forming in my right foot as we reached the old cemetery, and I was able to put out of my mind the feeling that hydrochloric acid was eating through my legs as we passed the apartment complex situated across the highway from my parents' neighborhood. Mike began to overtake me as we crossed the road. Almost synchronized, we darted down one road and turned left at full speed toward home. Without bothering to stop and catch our breath, we burst through the front door of my house, eager to make our way to the sanctuary of my bedroom.

"Whoa, whoa, whoa!" my dad yelled from his recliner positioned in front of the door. "What the hell are you two bangin' around so fast for?"

"We're . . . racing . . ." I barely managed to say between gulps of air as the sweat dripped off my arms and face and landed on the freshly cleaned carpet.

"Racing, huh?" my dad asked as he looked over at Mike. "So, who won?"

"Tie . . ." Mike squeaked out.

Dad considered us. Turning back to the television, he said, "Go get cleaned up. You're drippin' all over the place."

"Yessir," I answered, and the two of us half crawled to my room. As soon as we entered our safe haven, I closed and locked the door behind us. I began removing my shirt as Mike stumbled over to the window.

"Can you see it?" I asked him as he peeked through the blinds.

He turned to look at me. "Come see for yourself."

I gestured to him to make room so I could get a good look outside. My window faced almost the exact direction of the fire, and even from over a mile and a half away, we could see it: a thick cloud of black smoke rising high into the air, illuminated bright orange from below.

"FUC—" I barked as Mike quickly cupped his hand over my mouth.

"Shh!" he commanded. "They'll hear!"

"Fuck!" I whispered loudly. "Yeah, you're right. Okay, I'm sorry. Oh, man, *shit*! Shitshitshit!" I flung myself onto my water bed, causing it to slosh and gurgle wildly. "What the hell are we doing to do?"

"Nothing!" he whispered back. "We're going to do absolutely nothing."

"We gotta do *something*!"

"We *are* doing something—we're hiding!" he replied. "We're going to just stay here and hope to God no one saw us!"

I wasn't used to Mike being the calm one, but this time he definitely had the right idea. I mean, yeah, we just set fire to a portion of a major roadway, then sprinted down it with a billion cars screaming by in both directions . . . But hey, maybe we *did* make it back to my house unseen! Besides, I was in no position to be disagreeable.

We sat there, unable to comprehend the turn the evening had taken. I looked at Mike, who sat in my huge blue chair with his arms wrapped around his knees, which were pulled into his chest. Even though he didn't intend to, he broadcast emotion with each involuntary tic and rock of his body. Although we both felt guilty for what we'd done, our attention was much more focused on hoping we wouldn't have to go to jail.

"We were just . . . We just flicked some matches," I said to no one in particular.

"Yeah," he responded. "I feel like I have to, like . . ."

"Puke?" I asked.

He nodded.

"Yeah, I feel like I have to, too," I said. "I think instead I'm going to go take a piss." I got up and left the room. I couldn't help but look ahead to the living room at the television screen my father was watching. On it were images of a building on fire with a stream of water shooting at the flames. A small blue bar ran across the bottom of the screen, the left side of which said "Breaking Story" and the center of which said "Fire on Roadway."

My eyes shot wide open, and my stomach felt like it was about to leap from my esophagus. I ran back to the bedroom and slammed the door. "Ohshitohshitohshitohshit!"

"What!" Mike yelped, turning from the window. "What is it? Does your dad know?"

"Worse," I replied, and bade him come toward me.

He got up and we left the room, creeping down the hall to look at the TV. "Oh, shit!" Mike yelled as soon as he realized what he was looking at.

"What?" my mother yelled from the dining room. "Who said that?"

"Uh, I did, Mrs. Peacock," Mike said, wincing.

"And why are you saying such filthy things?" my mother asked.

He stammered for a moment, then said, "I stepped on a tack."

"A tack? Are you okay?" she asked, genuinely concerned.

"Yeah, I was . . . Oh, hey, what's going on there, on the television?"

My dad piped up. "Looks like there's a fire down the road there. That new Hooters . . . the one they're building near the car lot."

"Oh, my, that's dreadful," Mike said in his best Eddie Haskell voice. "Do they, uh, know how it started?"

I nudged him. Hard.

"Nah, they haven't said," my dad said. "Who knows. Could have been the heat, could have been one of those feminist groups setting it on fire."

We laughed very, very nervously. "Yeah, those nutty broads," I said. "They can be, you know. Nutty. Okay, off to bed with us!"

"So early?" my mother asked. "It's only ten-thirty. I'd assumed you boys would be up playing that Nintendo all night."

"No, ma'am," Mike answered. "We have to be up early for, uh . . . Sunday school, right?"

"You want to go to Sunday school?" my dad asked from the living room. "I thought you hated it."

"Well," Mike replied, "I guess I suddenly feel the need for the Lord to enter my life."

"Okay, good night!" I yelled, interjecting before Mike allowed his birth defect—severe stupidity—to kick in and sell us up the river. We ran back to my bedroom, turned off the lights, and proceeded to freak the hell out.

"Did you see the TV? We burned down the Hooters!" Mike said in the most exclaimed whisper I'd ever heard. "We are going to *jail*!"

"Dude, no," I said. "If they knew it was us, they'd have come for us by now, right?"

"Who knows?" he replied. "I don't know. Do you know?"

"No," I said. "But look at it this way—it's not like we committed murder or anything. Besides, it was an accident, right?"

"Yeah," he answered.

"They have to understand that, provided they ever find out. Oh, God, what if they find out?" Then it was Mike's turn to talk me down. This cycle continued intermittently throughout the evening as we lay there, silent in the dark, contemplating how fucked we might or might not be.

The next morning we all got up and had some breakfast. No one had come to the door in the middle of the night to arrest us. Mom and Dad hadn't said a word about the situation. The French toast was delicious, and it was sunny out. All, it seemed, was good with the world.

We got dressed in our Sunday best and my mom, dad, sister, Mike, and I piled into the huge pre-Sterno-burned Volkswagen Vanagon that made us famous wherever we went. We puttered down the road on the way to church. My dad usually went the back way to avoid traffic, but this time he decided to head down Tara Boulevard. "Uh, Dad?" I said.

"Yeah?"

"Why are you going this way today?" I asked.

"I wanna get a look at that Hooters," he replied.

"Oh." I looked at Mike, who looked as panicked as I did. "Any particular reason?"

"Just wanna see it," my dad answered. "I wanna see how bad it was."

Oh, it was bad. The entire framework that had been in progress definitely needed some renovation. There was a sizable square of blackened earth extending from the road to where the building was being constructed. All of the hay and seed they had laid was gone. It looked like the opening sequence from *Terminator 2*. All it was missing was a huge robotic foot to step down and crush a skull. But my parents said nothing. We were in the clear.

We finally started to relax as we arrived at church. Mike and I spent our morning asking intentionally difficult and/ or mean questions of the Sunday school teacher, who was obviously not qualified to handle our bullshit. We demanded to know why, if God is love, He would hate two men for loving each other, or how two of every animal could fit on a boat that was built in a few weeks, considering zoos didn't even have one millionth of the animal species in them and they took up several city blocks, or how the Ark could have been sealed with pitch, when pitch is tar and tar is old dinosaurs and dinosaurs weren't in the Bible. Stuff like that.

Class was dismissed, and we ate some cookies and drank some lemonade, then went to the eleven o'clock service, where we drew flipbook movies on the pages of the hymnals and made faces at our younger friends in the choir, causing them to lose their composure time and again. Offering was taken, hymns were sung (with certain words replaced to make them even more funny—there's much that can be done with songs called "Kneeling Before Him" and "The Son Is Come" and such).

Right before the sermon, our pastor always made the call for the congregation to ask that certain people be kept in our prayers that week. One was made for old Mrs. Hampton, whose husband had passed, and another was made for Julie Miles, who had broken her leg and couldn't compete in that weekend's cheerleading competition.

"Are there any others?" Pastor Roper asked.

"Yes," my father said, standing so as to be better heard.

"Brother Bill," the pastor said. "Who is your prayer request for?"

"My son and his friend Mike," he announced.

The calm I'd worked so hard to attain was gone. My bowels began to gurgle, and a shock went down my spine, forcing me to sit bolt upright. Judging from the sounds and movement I heard and felt next to me, the same thing had happened to Mike. Pastor Roper said, "All right, what will we be praying for this week for Joe and Mike?"

"Well," my father said, his crisp baritone ringing throughout the worship hall, "I ask that everyone pray for them to have the strength to turn themselves in to the police once we leave church today for setting that fire near Hooters last night."

The congregation gasped simultaneously. Mike and I sank down in our seats simultaneously. My dad's eyes looked in our direction and drilled holes through us simultaneously.

"How'd you—" I tried to ask.

"I knew the second you came running into the house that you'd done something stupid. And once the news report came on about the fire, I knew you two were behind it."

"But, Dad!" I said.

"Shut it, mister!" he yelled. His voice was normally very intimidating and booming, but inside this house of God, the acoustics made it sound like he was delivering the Word of the Almighty. "You mean to tell me you didn't do it? You're going to lie in a house of God?"

I sat stone silent. Not only could I not lie to my father, I especially couldn't do it in church.

"That's what I thought," he said, taking his seat.

I hung my head. I didn't need to look up to know that the eyes of the entire room were fixed on Mike and me, because I could feel their stares like lumps across my skin.

"Well, then," Pastor Roper said. "Let us pray." He began his standard prayer, asking for healing for the sick and alms for the poor and support for the weak milquetoast among the crowd. Then he added, "And I especially ask that you deliver both Mike and Joe into your guidance and shelter, dear Lord, because I have a feeling they're going to need it."

By that point in my life, I was finding that most prayers were severely overrated and mostly self-serving. But this one, I found appropriate.

After church, Dad drove the family to the police station, where he forced us out of the vehicle and marched us in to face the music. Oddly enough, Mike's parents were already in the waiting room, their faces fixed with a stern expression that could caramelize sugar. We were processed and remanded to our parents' custody until our court date. Our lawyer managed to work out a deal where we would have our records sealed and serve no time in exchange for—and this sucked—community service, and in the meantime, we'd have to attend counseling for pyromania and other assorted adolescent ailments.

We were specifically prevented from serving our community service together, which made the entire thing nearly unbearable. I chose to work at the Salvation Army for the majority of my community service, while Mike chose to help the elderly for part of his time and pick up trash on the side of the road with the rest. It didn't occur to me to ask if he ever found our matches.

CHAPTER 11

THE WAL-MART STORY

I was in my first (only) year of college and working for Roadway Package System on the overnight shift. RPS was a cheap knockoff of FedEx or UPS, only without all the customers and safety regulations, so we had at least fifteen employees out on workers' comp at any given time. What those guys were doing when they got hurt, I'll never know, because all I ever saw any of us do was basically sit around and move a few boxes here and there to create the illusion that we deserved seven dollars an hour. My job function consisted mostly of breaking open the occasional Nerf shipment and "playtesting" the toys all night. Sure, that stuff was meant for someone else, but the company's insurance would cover it. It was free Nerf, as far as I was concerned.

I decided to quit RPS one night (and by "quit," I mean to say that I physically demeaned the five-two late-night security guard by rubbing his head and calling him "cutie"; this was met rather quickly by the blunt end of his Maglite and a veritable honor guard of an escort out of the building).

Since I had lost my scholarship the very first quarter of school due to sleeping in class all day—because of late-night work, oddly enough—and I still had the futile intention to graduate, I was desperate for a late-night solution to my funds-to-tuition ratio. I had to do *something* for money. I thought about whoring my body out to dirty old men or selling hash made from yard grass and pencil shavings to high school kids, but I felt that as a future writer, I needed, for once in my life, to indulge in something truly dark and evil. Something from which immeasurable pain and embarrassment would come, so that I could have an experience to draw upon for inspiration in the future. Naturally, working at Wal-Mart was the first thing that came to mind.

I heard about the position from a friend of mine who, at his request, shall remain nameless. He was working the early-morning shift at the time. He explained that the electronics department needed a full-time employee on the overnight shift because the last person who worked there was caught masturbating to a Cindy Crawford workout tape at two A.M. while the other employees were in the break room. He could have gotten away with it; there were only two working security cameras in the whole store, one in the shoe department and the other at the customer service counter. But he chose to do it in the actual electronics department, where customers rarely—but sometimes do—shop.

I decided to give Wal-Mart a shot. I showed up for the pre-interview, which was basically a screening of a poorly produced security and procedure video. After that hearty thirty-minute nap, I was huddled into a corner of the room with a manager to begin the actual interview. Believe it or not, the interview process for Wal-Mart was pretty thorough. But they paid six dollars an hour—not as much as RPS, but still, a fortune at the time. It was worth it, since the job entailed wearing a blue smock, cleaning up after dullards, and answering, for the hundredth time in an hour, questions with answers that should be common sense.

After spending half my day on the interview and a drug test, then the two weeks it took to call the references and check out my background, I was accepted into the ranks of the Sam Walton elite: I became Joe "The Overnight Electronics Department Employee" Peacock.

To feel the full impact of such a job title, you must understand one crucial fact about life—and this fact will remain constant forever: No one normal works the overnight shift, *anywhere.* This is especially evident at Wal-Mart, where not only are you working overnight in a gigantic wasteland of a career path, you are doing so alongside people who clean department store floors and stock liquid Dawn dish soap and various salty Golden Flake snacks on shelves eight hours a night for a living, all in backwoods Georgia. These people weren't what one would consider to be members of the conversational elite.

My first few weeks on the job were rife with frustration. Because I was the new kid, and because I didn't belong in the social structure created by the employees, I ended up the victim of several pranks. I was told that the electronics person on the overnight shift had to cover for the pet department, which was at the opposite end of the store. I was also informed that during my downtime, I was to pitch in and help other departments stock their wares. It was common in those first few weeks to find me putting away stock that wasn't in my department while being paged back to my department or to the pet department every ten minutes for customers who, according to the employee who had paged me, had mysteriously just left.

Between stocking bars of Ivory, running to my department every ten minutes for phantom customers, and jogging over to the pet department to scoop fish for people who had no intention of purchasing them, I was pretty worn out every day when my shift ended. It was about a month before I found out that neither the shelf stocking nor the fish were my responsibility, and because my department was home to some of the most expensive and easily shopliftable items in the store, leaving it was a huge no-no. For all of my hard work and willingness to pitch in around the various departments, I received a big fat "needs improvement" on my first employee review.

Once I learned the truth about my extra duties and subsequently told those who'd asked me to do them to fuck themselves, things kind of leveled out and became simple for me. My daily routine ran as follows: I would arrive at the store at about ten P.M., help the third-shift person clean up, receive my stock about midnight, put it all away by one, and kick back and watch the brand-new digital satellite TV network or some of the latest releases on this new DVD technology while doing my homework until six A.M., when I left the store for class. I was becoming quite happy with my routine, despite the fact that I was surrounded by under-educated redneck mollusks who, while I was watching movies and the MTV2 network, were busy stocking detergent and mops that, a few months prior, they'd had a gullible college kid stock for them while they sat in the back room and turned the walls yellow with their three-pack-a-day tobacco habits. They kinda got pissed.

As time progressed, my manager started noticing discrepancies on my inventory reports every morning. Every night when I took over the shift, I had a little note that reminded me to check the battery count or verify that the film count matched up with the printout, because the rack was off by one or two. I would count and count again, and the counts would match exactly with the ones on the inventory printout I had just received from the inventory software. It baffled me why I had to keep verifying counts on the inventory my mananger had apparently counted that morning, but I chalked it up to busywork. I didn't spend too many cycles wondering why the almighty computer system at a discount department store was screwing up numbers. I figured, It's one goddamn roll of film in one Wal-Mart. It costs four bucks. Our profit last year was in the tens of millions.

But this was not a problem that faded away easily. More and more inventory began disappearing overnight from my department with no apparent cause. Over time, a roll of film turned into several rolls, which then graduated to video games, printer cartridges, and eventually a television. It truly made no sense to me, but every single evening I would get increasingly terse notes that stated that certain areas of our inventory were experiencing unaccounted-for reductions. I would watch the department like a hawk: Not a single customer made it in or out of the department on my shift without my gaze glued directly to them, and I never once saw any of them scanning the area nervously while shoving a television in their knickers. The morning-shift employee arrived at five-thirty for register count and shift change, so the theft couldn't be taking place between shifts. The disappearances were absolutely not happening. Nonetheless, inventory was vanishing from the shelves every morning and reappearing every evening when I started my shift.

One morning I was confronted by the overnight manager. I had no clue what was taking place. I walked over to the offending aisle of printer cartridges and demonstrated for him that the count matched EXACTLY with what was on his new morning printou . . . Hmm.

That was odd. It actually was off by one.

No one had even come into my department that evening. There was no way that any of the inventory could have left the department that evening. Something, somewhere, stank. Badly.

After a few days of asking around on the overnight shift, the morning manager received horrible reviews of my performance from the other employees. The part that fried my turkey was the fact that the overnight manager didn't speak out and back me up. He supported the claims of the overnight staff that not only was I lazy but I was also pilfering the stock for personal gain. I was furious! I did my job and I did it well! I mean, come on, how can one suck at watching free satellite TV?

I pleaded my case to the morning manger, to no avail. Unfortunately, when an entire overnight shift at a Wal-Mart hates you and their opinions get confirmation from the shift manager, anything you say to anyone who isn't there to see the comedy of errors probably won't believe you.

Which leads to a deeper, darker blemish on my record than my having worked at Wal-Mart: I, Joe the Peacock, was *fired* from Wal-Mart. I would say only a retard could get fired from Wal-Mart, but this isn't true: Even the door greeter with Down's syndrome who once bit a female customer and refused to let go was still employed. I was completely mortified.

I visited the store the following week to pick up my final paycheck. I met up with that nameless friend who'd suggested I take the job in the first place. He had heard all the rumors and gossip, and fortunately, he was pretty tight with a few of the overnight employees. Conversation ensued, and I discovered that, in an attempt to frame me for theft, some of those magnificent meatheads had been using the inventory gun to go in and scan items, then increase the inventory by one or two in the computer every morning, just in time for the inventory printout. That explained the unaccounted-for shrinkage in inventory. Pretty crafty, I must say, especially since at that time the inventory system didn't record what time a change was made if it had been entered manually. It only paid attention when things were scanned in from the truck or scanned out at the register and went out the door. And because I had no idea what was happening, I never thought to compare one count sheet to another.

The worst part of the entire conversation came when it was revealed that the overnight manager was in on the whole scam as well. He thought it was funny.

The only validation of my personal character came

when I asked him what I had done to piss them off so badly. He replied, "Dude, you didn't do anything. These are simple people who are not worthy of your hatred. You don't belong at a place like Wal-Mart. Everyone knows it. One day you will become a famous writer and amass a huge following. People will adore you and look at you as an influence for themselves and their children. Statues will be erected in your honor. A car will be named after you. You will be able to transmute lead into gold, and you will evolve into pure energy and understand the true nature of God." Or something like that—because he asked not to be named, he can't refute the quote.

Needless to say, I was a bit miffed. I felt that a company that would engage in these nefarious practices deserved some heavy-duty payback. After our conversation, I went home to plot out one of the most glorious plans for revenge ever conceived—well, maybe not ever conceived by, like, everyone, but definitely the most glorious ever conceived by me.

The day after Thanksgiving is, of course, the single busiest shopping day of the year. Every single Wal-Mart in the nation is swamped with parents hoping to find great deals on stupid toys that their children will destroy within four minutes of opening the package. This fact does not stop the parents from coming in droves to hand over their hard-earned money for the cheaply made knickknacks.

As the guy who'd set up just about everything in that department during the months I worked there, I had a few small advantages. For instance, I was the only one who knew the lockout codes for the satellite system (then called USSB), which was located in the demo cabinet. Along with the satellite system was the demo DVD player (which could also play AVI video CDs that could be made on a personal computer) and demo VCR. Incidentally, I was the only employee who even knew there were keys for that cabinet, because when I'd set it up, I'd grabbed the keys and put them on my key ring. We never locked the cabinet, so I quickly forgot that the keys even existed. I happened to keep the keys after I left the company (the only copy of those keys). I also happened to be the only one with all the passwords to all the demo PCs in the department.

My major advantage was the knowledge that while there were two department phones on the counters near the registers, there was a third line that was active but unused under the main CD rack in the center of the department. Back in those days, the phone/intercom system wasn't digital; it was your basic everyday analog line.

Thanksgiving night, the store closed for the evening so the employees could go home and have dinner with the family. But they reopened after midnight for employees to prep for the upcoming onslaught of bargain hunters. I sneaked into the store through the gardening department and began working on my plan, which was especially easy, since the morning manager had never gotten around to filling my position, and almost everyone except the custodians showed up late due to the holiday. I thought it was going to be difficult, but no—the store was my playground.

First, I glided over to the unlocked demo machine cabinet. I attacked the satellite system, locking out every channel except for the Hot Network, a hard-core pornography channel for which I then ordered a full day of programming.

I inserted in the DVD player a special AVI video CD I had burned on my home machine, and then I put a special VHS tape into the VCR. I turned off all the units, so the TV screens showed only black. I turned the volume on every TV to max, locked the demo cabinet, and stole all the remotes for the systems from the front drawer.

I moved over to the PCs and changed a few settings, then rebooted them to lock in the passwords. Finally, I took a cordless telephone from the department and plugged it in to the aforementioned vacant store phone jack under the CD rack, hiding the base of the unit with boxes of inventory. I ran over to the pharmacy section to plug in the remote charger and phone receiver so it would be fully charged for the next morning. Everything in place, I left the store with a gigantic smile on my face.

Six A.M. rolled around. The newspaper flyers had advertised special early-bird prices for certain items for weeks on end, and droves of bargain shoppers packed the store. There were lines for each department, lines for checking out . . . It was a madhouse. During the chaos, I breezed through the store, blending in with the crowds. Since the morning crew was on staff, not a single person recognized me. I went over to my rigged electronics department to do a final survey of the area. All the televisions were on, screens black, with a small message at the bottom of the screen that said "signal unavailable." All of the demo PCs had rolled over to their screensavers, which scrolled in blue text on a red background I AM A LUCKY COMPUTER! TAKE ME HOME! Moving the mouse or using the keyboard would not disable the screensaver, since it had a password. Everything looked ready.

I ran over to my secret hiding area in the pharmacy, the only department not completely ravished by the holiday shopping crowd, and pulled out the cordless phone. The batteries were good, and when I entered the code for an overhead page and blew into the receiver, my puffs were clearly audible over the intercom. It was time for the festivities to begin.

Using the paging system I had just hijacked, I announced in a clear and resounding tone: "Greetings, Wal-Mart holiday shoppers! Thank you so much for coming out this wonderful day to take advantage of our special deals! One of our unadvertised specials is taking place right now! For the next thirty minutes in the electronics department, if you see a computer with a message scrolling across that says 'I am a lucky computer! Take me home!' that model is seventy percent off the already low sale price! These computers are first come, first serve, so hurry to the electronics department, and as always, thank you for shopping at Wal-Mart."

The stampede began. I made my way along with hordes of bargain hunters to the electronics department to witness the lucky shoppers search for the computers that were on "sale." What a lucky day! Every single machine had a demo model scrolling the magic phrase! I figured that Wal-Mart's policy was to honor any advertised price, and in-store announcements qualified as an advertisement, so my ploy would put a gigantic dent in their normal operational activity. But that was frosting on my cake. My actual intention was not to screw Wal-Mart on the price of their crappy Acer and Packard Bell computers; it was to build an audience.

As the department reached a capacity bordering on critical,

I pulled out my stolen remotes for the demo units and turned on all three of them. The top row of televisions, at full volume, flipped to images from the satellite system, which was locked on hard-core pornography; the middle tier showed images from the VCR, which contained a movie entitled *Where the Boys Aren't: Sorority Sleepover;* and the bottom row played footage from the DVD system, which contained a video CD full of downloaded German *Scheiße* films from the darkest reaches of Usenet.

There is no way I can describe the resulting chaos better than you are probably imagining it, so I will leave it alone, mentioning only that I barely managed to crawl out of the store because I was doubled over from laughter. What a happy holiday season I had that year.

I heard later from my nameless friend that the "wall o' filth" played at full volume for nearly an hour, since the department was so packed with spectators that employees could barely move through to the demo cabinet. They obsessed over unlocking it instead of simply turning off the televisions. Overall, the panic and unrest went on for half the day. Months later, after I was well past my balloon-twisting career and starting into the dot-com world, my nameless friend brought up the prank and, through his chuckles, told me the employees still hadn't figured out how I'd hijacked the paging system. I was tempted to go to the store and see if the cordless phone was still plugged in so I could pull the entire stunt once again.

The best part of it all: The store accidentally paid me for another two weeks after I had been fired. A few weeks after mailing me the check for the work I didn't clock in for, they sent a letter explaining that there had been an error in the payroll system and requesting that I send the money back. I wrote the word "Scheiße" with a chocolate bar on the letter and mailed it back, wondering if they would get the joke. I then put the money in a tech-heavy stock portfolio that, in 2001, tanked. Oh, well. Easy come, easy go.

ABOUT THE STORIES

The first seven chapters of this book ("Doing the Gay," "Never Saw That One Coming . . . ," "The Hospital Is No Place to Spend Your Birthday," "1-800-STALKER," "Where's Your Sense of Adventure?" "I Never Really Was the Outdoors Type," and "Sorry, Deer") were voted on by the readers of the Web site where this book was created, mentallyincontinent.com. The winning stories for each round of voting became the chapters in the book you're holding. If you hate one (or all) of them, blame the voters.

As such, each of those chapters has three or four other stories that didn't make it through the voting but are very deserving of your attention and are still on the Web site. I encourage you to head to the site, give them a read, and let me know what you think.

"Just Hangin' Around," "Just Visiting," and "The Wal-Mart Story" are older stories from my first book that the Web site members felt were too important to leave out of this book, so they forced me to add them. You can also read all the stories from the first book (all the stories that became chapters, as well as those that did not) on the site. So if you like what you've read here, go there and like that stuff too.

"Oooh, Burned!" was added because I wanted it in here. My call. Sorry again, Dad.

AN AFTERWORD BY
BRENT JOHNSON,
NO APOLOGIES! PRESS

I had asked my friend and certified Japanese drink expert, Brent Johnson, to do a foreword for my first book. He took forever to get it to me, and by the time he did, another friend had already filled the void. But it was a very sweet and wonderful foreword, and I'd be remiss if I didn't give it the chance to shine that it deserves. So it's now an after-word, if there is such a thing. And if there isn't . . . well, there is now.

I came across mentallyincontinent.com long before I ever communicated with Joe Peacock. I hated it. HATED. IT. I recognized what Joe was doing, and it gnawed upon my dead-and-tiny-yet-still-envious heart—he was creating something huge, something different, something special. Something I wish I had the endurance and heart to do.

I help run what my partners and I have officially termed a third-rate humor site, and I know from experience how hard it can be to refresh your site with new content on a continuous basis. But because it is third-rate humor, I don't have to hurt when someone rips it apart. It's easy to shrug nonchalantly and to "not care."

But I gotta admit, whenever someone says "Nice stuff," an electrical surge streaks through me. Which just goes to show what a coward I am—taking the good and shunting away the bad. Which just goes to show what a brave bastard Joe is.

Mentally Incontinent can't hide. It's in your face. The author is what makes it work—or not work—and he can't duck away from your criticism (or your criticism's inbred cousin, insult). Maybe Joe didn't know what he was getting into when he started, but the fact that he's continued with the Mentally Incontinent projects is nothing short of miraculous.

Or maybe it's not miraculous. Maybe he's simply got what it takes to succeed in his gambit. I don't know that I could live up to it—and if I can't, most of you can't, either.

Whatever the case, Joe's the hardest-working man on the Internet. Or one of them. I haven't met anyone else who works harder, anyway. Oh, and he's funny as hell, too— which makes all of the above worth writing.

THANKS

I know that the thank-you bits in books are usually short and sweet, but this is my first-ever book published by a big house, so I'm going to take the opportunity to thank everyone I've ever wanted to thank. I'm not passing up this chance.

Very first and foremost, to every single reader, voter, and editor on mentallyincontinent.com. You guys are the reason I'm doing what I'm doing, and I love you all. I'm not going to come to your house and play Wii and eat Oreos with you or anything, but I still love you.

To Drew Curtis, who has given me pretty much every break I've ever gotten, and who introduced me to Woodford Reserve, the best writing fuel ever.

To Mike Crawford, without whom life since the tenth grade would have had much less fun and good music.

To Hillary Terrel, for taking a chance on me, and to Patrick Mulligan, for keeping that chance alive. And to E. Beth Thomas, who faced the Sisyphean task of trying to fix my typos and errors.

To Jeremy Halvorsen, for keeping my shit straight, and for being an honest voice even when the last thing I wanted to hear was honesty.

To Michal Wallace, without whom I never would have started the Mentally Incontinent Web site in the first place.

To my dear, dear sister, Virginia Hall, who takes the only photographs of me that don't make me look like a hideous monster.

To Todo at ABT Tattoo in McDonough, Georgia, for the amazing Akira sleeve tattoo. Everyone should collect at least one Todo piece in their lives. And to Jeremiah "JET" Turner for my super fanboy leg tats.

To Jessie Rylett, Kelsey Marryskows, Saralee Briley, Amy Grace, Liss Jenssen, and Alan "Colin" Ainsworth, who are all incredible brats and who make the best suggestions on stories.

To Doug Stephenson at Downtown Comics, who gave me the single best compliment I've ever had: "No matter what anyone else says, you should know that your writing IS masculine."

To Henry Rollins, Dave Sim, Frank Miller, Neil Gaiman, Evan Dorkin, Alan Moore, Gordon Rennie, Martin Emond, Katsuhiro Otomo, Masamune Shirow, Garth Ennis, Brian Wood, Stephen King, Dave Barry, Carlton "Chuck D" Ridenhour, Cee-Lo Green, Seth Godin, and Scott McCloud—inspiration is the greatest gift one can give another, and you all gave it to me in spades. On the off chance that any of you ever read this, know that you made this thing happen.

To my parents, to whom I promised the dedication of this book but yet again let down (don't worry, they're used to it).

To Field Notes notebooks (www.fieldnotesbrand.com) for making the only Joe-proof grid-line memo pads on the planet.

To Jack Link's Beef Jerky and Red Bull. You both know why.

And to my beautiful wife, whom I've already thanked in the dedication and is all huffy about not being in the "Thanks" and is now just being greedy. Quit reading over my shoulder.

REACH OUT
AND TWEET SOMEONE

Got thoughts or opinions on this book or other stuff I've done? Please feel free to contact me:

Web site: http://www.joethepeacock.com
E-mail: joe@mentallyincontinent.com
Facebook: http://www.facebook.com/joe.peacock
Twitter: http://www.twitter.com/joethepeacock
AIM: joethepeacock
GTalk: joethepeacock@gmail.com
Smoke signals: *puff* *puff* (pause) *puff*

ABOUT THE AUTHOR

J oe Peacock runs the Web site www.mentallyincontinent
.com, writes books, plays semiprofessional football,
fights in mixed martial arts tournaments, and draws pretty
pictures for Web sites. He has cats and a wife he does not
deserve, and lives in Atlanta.